MW00377830

Copyright © 2000 Sleeping Bear Press

All rights reserved. No part of this book may be reproduced in
any manner without the express written consent of the
publisher, except in the case of brief excerpts in critical reviews
and articles. All inquiries should be addressed to:

Sleeping Bear Press
310 North Main Street
P.O. Box 20
Chelsea, MI 48118
www.sleepingbearpress.com

Printed and bound in Canada.

10 9 8 7 6 5 4 3 2 1

Library of Congress Cataloging-in-Publication Data
Brown, Scott.
The major : 7 days at golf's greatest championship / by Scott
Brown and the staff of the Monterey County herald.
p. cm.
ISBN 1-58536-027-9
1. U.S. Open (Golf tournament) (2000 : Pebble Beach, Calif.)
2. Pebble Beach Golf Links (Pebble Beach, Calif.) I. Monterey
County herald. II. Title

GV970.3.U69 B76 2000
796.352'66—dc21
00-046394

The MAJOR

7 Days at Golf's Greatest Championship

By Scott Brown and
the staff of the *Monterey County Herald*

Sleeping Bear Press

"If golf was art, then
Payne was the color.
The challenge is not to
forget Payne. And not
just Payne the golfer,
but Payne the person."

— Paul Azinger

"This is the place I started in many ways. About 40 years later, it's a pretty fitting place to stop. If I was going to pick a spot to play my last U.S. Open, it would be Pebble Beach."

— Jack Nicklaus

"Any superlative
would still be an
understatement. He's
a poet, a virtuoso,
an artist. It must
be a dream."
— Ernie Els, on Tiger Woods

Foreword

In 1999, Clint Eastwood, Dick Ferris, Arnold Palmer and I, along with 100 other individuals, became custodians of Pebble Beach. I say "custodians" rather than "owners," as the meeting of land and sea that is Pebble Beach is meant for everyone to enjoy and possess in some way. The essence of this great place is that for all its unmatched splendor it still remains a public course.

Never has this sentiment of accessibility been more evident than at the 100th U.S. Open, held at Pebble Beach in June 2000. For one week, we reveled in golf's illustrious past, compelling present, and boundless future. We came to celebrate a game and left having seen its history rewritten. For those who enjoy sport — any sport — no explanation is necessary. For those who do not, no explanation is possible.

For days, weeks, and perhaps years after the event, this centennial and millennial Open will be remembered for the way Tiger Woods went about winning his first national championship and third major title. His win by a margin of 15 strokes was the most dominating four-round performance in the history of golf.

The week also featured a final U.S. Open bear hug for Jack Nicklaus, a tearful farewell to Payne Stewart, and the glorious return of a native son, Bobby Clampett. Never have so many stories coincided so richly in one event and been played out in such colorful fashion.

When all was said and done, we were simply grateful that this drama could unfold on the game's greatest stage, Pebble Beach. What transpired over seven days here became as elemental to the place as its rolling fairways and crashing waves. Like Pebble Beach's indescribable surroundings, the 100th U.S. Open is something to be remembered forever.

— Peter Ueberroth

Contents

Introduction

A fishing boat diesels its way down the channel and into Monterey Bay. Her iron hull is stained by mossy spots of rust and there's a ragged feel to her wheelhouse. The rungs of her ladders are worn by the palms of hard-luck fishermen past, and a deep scent of oil and something more raw hovers in her joints and corners.

Her prow begins to split the sea. A young man stands on the stern of his boat, with his home sliding away behind him, the onset of morning before him. He mulls the irony. Something like this institution has existed for so long, and yet today he owns it. It is his moment to love or lose.

A few miles back, over the mountains and into the Del Monte Forest, a young man silhouettes against the morning mist. Everyone will come to see him, yet he is there before any of them, forging his rough-hewn swing. He, too, mulls the irony. Five hundred years of legend and lore could not prepare the game for the likes of him. The institution in which he walks will never be the same, as he has designs to scatter its annals into the Pacific wind. It is his moment.

More than 200 years before, poet William Blake placed immortal glory on the shoulders of "The Tyger." For one week, the young man would burn as brightly as the poem suggested, shouldering the weight of immortality.

CHAPTER ONE

The History

*The return of the U.S. Open
to Pebble Beach stirred memories
of three of the championship's greatest shots.*

Jack Nicklaus' sizzling 1-iron shot from the 17th tee bounced off the flagstick and secured him the 1972 U.S. Open title.

Echoes of the past

During their final practice round for the 2000 U.S. Open, three golfers were walking down a long stretch of fairway on Pebble Beach's gargantuan 573-yard 14th hole. An older gentleman standing behind the spectators' ropes pulled a canvas sack from his jacket and removed three balls.

Giggling, he whistled to the golfers and sheepishly rolled the balls out at their feet. The players discovered the balls were gutta-perchas, the kind used by players in the late nineteenth century.

All three players had already hit their regular balls, distributing them around the circumference of the green 275 yards away. Taking the antique hand-molded "gutties," their approach shots fell nearly 125 yards short of their first ones. Instead of putting, the players ended up hitting 7-irons to the green, then scrambling for par or worse.

More than any other sport, golfers have an abiding respect for their game's history. In the four days upcoming, the three golfers who struck blasts from the past on No. 14 hoped to make a little history of their own.

A debt of gratitude

Before they braced for the toughest test in golf, each U.S. Open contestant owed a debt of gratitude to Samuel Morse. It was in 1915 that Morse was hired as overseer of the property that is now known as Pebble Beach Golf Links. Morse immediately decided to throw out plans for a subdivision of 50-by-100 lots along an astonishing piece of coastline off Carmel Bay. In its place, Morse configured a course taking full advantage of the world's greatest meeting of land and water. It winds through cypress, pine, and oak trees, over Stillwater Cove and along the Cliffs of Doom, a three-hole gauntlet of par 4s that can make or break a round and a career.

Through the U.S. Open, Pebble Beach has long made a habit of identifying the best golfer of each era. In the process were distilled some of the greatest final rounds and three of the most memorable shots in golf history.

1972: A 1-iron for the ages

Sweeping winds turned the final round of the 1972 U.S. Open — Pebble Beach's first as host of the championship — into a survival test, as Jack Nicklaus battled the gales and rival Arnold Palmer. In a dramatic split-screen television image that signaled an advancement in the broadcasting of golf, Palmer missed a chance to catch or even pass Nicklaus, erring on a 10-foot birdie putt on No. 14 while Nicklaus

Jack Nicklaus celebrated his third Open championship at Pebble Beach in 1972.

made an 8-foot bogey putt on No. 12. With Nicklaus clinging to a one-shot lead, Palmer bogeyed the next two holes en route to a 76.

Nicklaus had a three-shot lead over Bruce Crampton when he stepped to the 17th tee. Strangely, three shots was exactly the lead Nicklaus said he'd had in a recurring dream on the eve of the final round.

"I arrived at the 17th tee every time with a comfortable three-stroke lead," Nicklaus told *Golf* magazine, "but there was no way I could make par there with the cup cut left of the hump in the green. Finally, I decided to take the bogey and go on to 18. There, now leading by only two shots, all I could do was hit the tee shot either into the ocean on the left or out-of-bounds on the right.

"I tried the driver, then the 3-wood, then the 1-iron,

> *"Watching everybody just sort of demolish themselves, I just kept playing golf, kept playing golf. And I played pretty well."*
>
> — Jack Nicklaus

then went through them all again and either dunked the ball or knocked it OB every time. Finally I couldn't stand it any longer and leaped out of bed."

Nicklaus' wife, Barbara, asked him what was wrong.

"I told her, 'I've played the 17th and 18th holes for two hours, and I can't play them. I don't know what I'm going to do if I get there this afternoon with a three-stroke lead, but I'm sure not going to play them again right now.' It was the worst dream I've ever had about golf — just awful."

Nicklaus stared into a howling wind as he stood on the 17th tee with an actual three-shot lead. This time, he didn't play for bogey. Nicklaus unleashed a low, sizzling 1-iron that cut through the wind, bounced off the flagstick and stopped six inches from the hole.

Nicklaus tapped in for birdie, effectively securing a hold on his third Open championship. He shot a final-round 74 and finished at 2-over 290, three ahead of Crampton.

"Very, very difficult conditions," Nicklaus said. "Very windy. Very dry.

"Watching everybody just sort of demolish themselves, I just kept playing golf, kept playing golf. And I played pretty well."

1982: For the ages

"It's a pleasure to be in your time."

In 1982, ABC's Jack Whitaker delivered those words to Jack Nicklaus when it looked as if the greatest golfer of any era was about to win a record fifth U.S. Open at his favorite course. The laurels turned out to be premature, however, as moments later, Tom Watson struck perhaps the most famous shot in golf history.

When Watson arrived at the 218-yard 17th hole in the final round, he was tied for the Open lead with Nicklaus at 4-under par.

Having carded a Sunday 69, there was nothing Nicklaus could do but wait and watch on television as Watson played two of Pebble Beach's most difficult holes. Watson's 2-iron tee shot hooked left of the 17th green into heavy rough. He was less than 20 feet from the hole, facing a nasty shot from deep grass with a downhill lie to a slippery green that sloped away from him.

> ## *"Get it close, hell — I'm going to sink it."*
> — Tom Watson

It looked to be an impossible shot, but Watson had caught a big break. Instead of nestling into what Watson described as the "gnarly grass," his tee shot wound up with "a little bit of cushion under it."

As Watson took his sand wedge out of his bag, his caddie, Bruce Edwards, encouraged him to "get it

Caddie Bruce Edwards congratulates Tom Watson on the shot of a lifetime, as Watson's chip-in for birdie on No. 17 gave him his first and only U.S. Open title.

close" and save par.

Watson had a better idea.

"Get it close, hell — I'm going to sink it," he told Edwards.

Watson opened the blade of his club, took a hard swing and popped a shot high into the air. It landed softly on the front edge of the green and started rolling toward the hole, breaking right.

When his ball disappeared into the hole, Watson raised both fists above his head and ran around the left side of the green in a short victory lap.

"At that moment I could have long-jumped all the way to Tokyo Harbor," Watson wrote in an article for *Golf Digest.*

Watson followed that miraculous birdie with a birdie at the par-5 18th, capping a two-shot victory over Nicklaus.

When Nicklaus arrived to shake Watson's hand, he smiled and leaned into the victor's ear and said, "You little son of a bitch, you're something else."

It was the third installment in the Watson-Nicklaus saga. Number 1 came at Augusta in 1977, when Watson battled Nicklaus down the stretch to win the first of his two Masters titles — with a birdie on 17, incidentally. Number 2 came later that summer at Turnberry in Scotland, when Watson captured the British Open's claret jug in a furious head-to-head duel, 65-65 in the third round, 65-66 in the last round — again, with the decisive birdie coming on the 17th hole.

Watson's chip-in ranked in history with two similar shots that helped decide major championships. The first was in the 1962 Masters, when Palmer used a wedge to hole out beside the 16th, allowing him to reach a play-off with Gary Player and Dow Finsterwald. The second was the chip shot Lee Trevino sank on the next-to-last hole at Muirfield in the 1972 British Open. Nicklaus, shooting for the third leg of the Grand Slam, was the victim there — on the 17th hole, of course.

1992: Kite flies higher

There was a moment during the final round of the 1992 U.S. Open when, despite 28 players still remaining on the course, the championship was all but conceded to a fair-haired Scotsman named Colin Montgomerie. At the 18th green, just as Montgomerie holed out for an even-par 288, Nicklaus even told him, "Congratulations on your first U.S. Open victory."

At that very moment, 42-year-old Tom Kite, the reigning "Best Player to Never Win a Major," stood on the seventh hole's elevated tee box, trying to keep his balance in 40 mph wind. The gales were turning Pebble Beach, with its rock-hard greens and high rough, into a torture chamber.

> *"My first thought was, 'Yeah, Watson did it,' but he only had one more hole to play, and I still had the entire golf course left."*
>
> — Tom Kite

How bad was it? Well, 20 players that day shot in the 80s. Scott Simpson shot 88, Mark Brooks 84, Payne Stewart and Davis Love III 83, Gil Morgan 81, and Paul Azinger 80.

After sinking a 25-foot birdie putt at the par-5 sixth, Kite was even-par for the final round and 3-under for the tournament.

Pebble Beach's seventh hole stretches only 106 yards. From the elevated tee, the green looks close enough to touch. On a calm day, a full wedge would fly over the green and into the Pacific Ocean.

But on this day, Kite was hitting into the wind. So he pulled out his 6-iron and tried to punch a shot through the air current.

Good idea. Bad execution.

Kite's shot sailed long and left of the green, settling into thick rough behind a bunker.

Tom Kite finally cast off the "can't win a major" curse when he won the 1992 U.S. Open, holing out a chip on No. 7, then clinging to victory through brutal wind that has become the stuff of legend.

Kite found his ball in a brutal lie. Yet he hit a delicate shot that barely carried the bunker, landed on the green and headed toward the hole.

Kite's ball hit the flagstick and disappeared into the cup for a birdie.

"My first thought was, 'Yeah, Watson did it,' but he only had one more hole to play, and I still had the entire golf course left," Kite said later.

Kite played those final 11 holes in 1-over par, finishing at even-par 72 for the round and 3-under 285 for the tournament, two ahead of Jeff Sluman and three ahead of Montgomerie.

Kite won 19 times on the PGA Tour and earned more than $10 million, the most of his era. However, he'd struggled in the majors, faltering in 19 previous Opens and suffering the indignity of not having an invitation to the 1992 Masters, despite having won five tournaments and more than $2 million since 1989, when he was the Tour's leading money winner with $1.4 million.

Finally, he was free of the curse that had plagued him.

"No one was more disappointed in my performances in majors than I was," Kite said. "It bugged the living daylights out of me. Now, no one can say I'm not a true winner."

CHAPTER TWO

Getting
the Open

*Pebble Beach and the USGA shared a vision
for producing a centennial championship
unlike any that had gone before.*

A U.S. Open banner is unfurled above the U.S. Open Village in the days leading up to the event.

An Open notion

The idea was tantalizing, even in 1992. The 100th U.S. Open. The year 2000. Pebble Beach. The U.S. Open, you see, is the confessional of golf. It is where the game's greats reveal themselves like nowhere else. Maybe it's the tradition that brings it out, or perhaps the world's focus. Maybe it's the competition, or the course conditions. Nonetheless, the U.S. Open is the place golfers bring their best games and are revealed at their basest level.

Imagine: One hundred years of history condensed into three days of tale-telling, lie-swapping and gamesmanship, followed by four days of spectacular shotmaking. And what better place for it all to unfold than Pebble Beach, the cradle of American golf? The place would serve as a truth serum for golfers, with its beauty and history prying open their hearts and inspiring a heightened level of play.

One look at the photos on the walls of The Lodge at Pebble Beach tells you this is a place that brings generations together, sparking memories and inviting comparisons. There's Arnie on one wall talking with Jack. There's Jones on another, and Hogan and Sarazen at the far end.

A greenskeeper gives a final trim before the event begins.

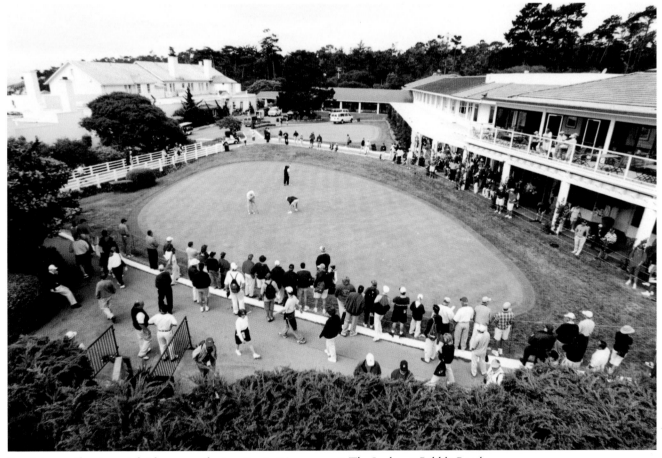

Spectators gather to watch players on the practice putting green at The Lodge at Pebble Beach.

The footbridge on Pebble Beach's new fifth hole was designed to resemble the striking Bixby Creek Bridge in nearby Big Sur.

Kayaks line the water's edge alongside the pier at Stillwater Cove by the Pebble Beach Club.

It is a public place, after all — one for the champions and the never-weres, the legends and the caddies, the barristers and the bartenders, the former presidents and the innkeepers. One and all can pay quiet homage or raise rowdy toasts to the intriguing, addicting game of golf.

Best of all, Pebble Beach unveils itself slowly, starting like a lamb and ending like a lion. It is a symbol of how golf is revealed by degrees. Pebble Beach's first three holes are ordinary. Holes 4, 5 and 6 have golfers holding their breath. The seventh hole, a 106-yard par 3 scented with salt and barking seals and wondrous hills, is the place's soul. By the time they're standing over their second shot on No. 8, a 175-yard approach over yawning oceanside cliffs 150 feet above the sea, the golfer is guaranteed to be experiencing a seminal moment.

So how could it be arranged that the centennial U.S. Open would come to Pebble Beach?

The meetings begin

It was Tuesday, June 16, two days before the 1992

U.S. Open was to begin at Pebble Beach. Most of the attention centered on whether Tom Watson could duplicate his miraculous win of 1982, or if Mark O'Meara, who just seemed to win every time he showed up at Pebble Beach, would finally take the national championship he'd long coveted.

But United States Golf Association executive director David Fay was neither reflecting on the past, nor overly concerned about the present. He was already looking toward the future.

Fay met with Paul Spengler of the Pebble Beach Company, who was the general chairman of the 1992 Open, and asked if he would consider hosting the championship again — but sooner than the 10-year rotation Pebble Beach had been following from 1972 through 1992. The USGA was thinking ahead to its centennial, and wanted a field of play that would provide a fitting backdrop. Pebble Beach was their singular desire.

Spengler expressed an immediate interest. In fact, he had already daydreamed about how he might give the Open a greater sense of grandeur.

After their meeting, Fay and Spengler went back to the task at hand. But the seeds for an unparalleled golf spectacle had been planted. By the time Tom Kite's gritty play down the stretch on Sunday resulted in his winning the 92nd U.S. Open, the clock was already ticking on the championship's return to Pebble Beach.

The following spring, representatives from the USGA met with a group from Pebble Beach in what Spengler said were "friendly conversations" about the Open's return to the Monterey Peninsula. The USGA's first choice for the 2000 Open remained Pebble Beach. Fay's message was clear: "We would like to invite you to host the 100th U.S. Open."

An unorthodox arrangement

Spengler went to work outlining a plan that would work best for Pebble Beach, all the while creating a vision for what he felt could be golf's greatest championship.

Pebble Beach organizers believed the company would be better positioned if it owned the rights to the entire event, rather than leasing out their facility for the week. The difference could mean millions of dollars, so Pebble Beach proposed paying an event fee to the USGA up front, rather than following the traditional protocol of the USGA paying Pebble Beach a fixed amount for using the site.

Imagine: One hundred years of history condensed into three days of tale-telling, lie-swapping, and gamesmanship, followed by four days of spectacular shotmaking.

At the time, the USGA considered this an unorthodox means of operating an Open, though organizers of the 1999 championship at Pinehurst, N.C., eventually put together a similar deal. It meant Pebble Beach would be responsible for more than any host site in the past, but Spengler's team felt it was crucial to their strategy. All of the event's infrastructure, staffing, marketing, and merchandising would be under the Pebble Beach umbrella — a heady strategy, to say the least.

Roughly 35,000 tickets would be sold to the event per day — an increase of 10,000 tickets per day over 1992 — and Pebble Beach would attempt to up its number of corporate tents from 8 to 40.

By June 1993, Pebble Beach and the USGA had closed negotiations, and on the Wednesday of the championship that year at Baltusrol Golf Club in Springfield, N.J., the announcement was made: the 100th U.S. Open was to be held at Pebble Beach.

The hottest ticket

Just how hot were tickets for the 100th U.S. Open? White hot.

Tickets became available immediately after Payne Stewart dropped his final putt at Pinehurst No. 2 in June 1999. Within 24 hours, over 100,000 fans submitted applications to attend the centennial Open at Pebble Beach in 2000. Using a lottery system, which was first implemented in 1998 due to high demand, the United States Golf Association selected 32,500 individuals who would be fortunate enough to hold daily passes for the event.

"It's the best ticket in sport this year," USGA president Trey Holland said. "Even better than the World Series or the Olympics. It's a chance to be involved with history and to perhaps watch (Jack) Nicklaus walk up No. 18 one more time."

Originally, daily tickets for the Open went for $65, and a weeklong pass was $275. Tickets for practice rounds were $35.

But the relative scarcity of tickets created an open-market frenzy two months shy of the 2000 Open, with passes for the week being sold through ticket brokers for as much as $5,000.

"I've never seen the value of a ticket multiply so many times over," said Andrew Clarke of Event Masters Inc., a ticket-brokering firm based in Atlanta. "It speaks to the unparalleled popularity of golf right now, and to the magnetism of Pebble Beach.

"At the outset of 2000, I'd not have thought the Open would be the hottest thing going. But it's by far the most difficult ticket to get this year. The demand has been unparalleled."

CHAPTER THREE

Getting Ready

Certainly championship officials could make changes to Pebble Beach's customary layout. But should they?

A Pebble Beach groundskeeper cuts a new hole on the 18th green. Hole locations were among the topics discussed on numerous visits to Pebble Beach by USGA officials.

Preparations for the U.S. Open on and off the course reached a fever pitch in the days leading up to the event. Here, workers prepare for a ceremony on the fifth hole.

Change for the better?

When all is said and done, the United States Golf Association wants players to go to bed visualizing the U.S. Open layout the way Ahab visualized the whale.

The greens are to be capricious, the bunkers cavernous, and the rough carnivorous. Balls should roll off the putting surfaces like water off a leaf; the fairways should ramble like a sloping high-rise without handrails.

In short, it should be the greatest test in golf, with the world's premier player emerging as champion from the four-day gauntlet. The question in 2000 with the Open coming to Pebble Beach was the following: How much challenge would the USGA need to manufacture to create the desired effect, and how much would Mother Nature do herself?

Certainly, the USGA could change Pebble Beach. But should it? To overly alter Pebble Beach would be as presumptuous as finding wrong notes in Beethoven's Ninth; pointing out to da Vinci a flaw in the Mona Lisa; calling Hemingway for a rewrite.

Landscape artist Francis McComas once called Pebble Beach "the greatest meeting of land and water in the world." Contributing to Pebble's panoramic, Technicolor appeal, of course, is the ocean blue.

The game of golf was born on seaside linksland in Scotland, so it was only appropriate that the USGA chose to bring its centennial Open to a course with an ocean view. The sea isn't just a backdrop at Pebble Beach, but a physical presence as well. The world's largest lateral hazard is in play on no fewer than 17 shots the golfer must hit at Pebble. Ten of its 18 holes run alongside the Pacific, leaving the fairways exposed to sea breezes that can become ocean gales at the drop of a flagstick.

"I cannot hit it out of the rough on this golf course, unless I get lucky. For me, it's impossible."

— Tom Watson

"There's an old Scottish saying that 'If there's nae wind, there's nae gowf,' and it's a sentiment with which I heartily concur," Jack Nicklaus said. "It's not that I dislike playing in calm conditions; it's just that a good

All traces of golfers who have gone before are erased from the bunkers at Pebble Beach Golf Links as part of the meticulous pre-U.S. Open grooming of the course.

Grandstands for spectators and scaffolds for TV cameras lined the panoramic seventh hole.

wind sorts out the good golfers and the true champions. I can't deny that tight fairways, high rough, and firm greens place stringent demands on a golfer during the U.S. Open or U.S. Amateur, but when the wind also becomes a factor then the difficulty increases dramatically."

Preserving history

It was also critical that the USGA not tamper with the historical precedent Pebble had established as host of three previous Opens. In 1972, '82 and '92, Pebble Beach established itself as American golf's ultimate standard-bearer, each time revealing the era's top golfer — Nicklaus, Tom Watson, and Tom Kite, respectively — as the winner.

"More than in any Open year, I hope the USGA carefully considers whatever alterations it makes to Pebble Beach," Nicklaus said. "To me, it's the most complete test of golf as it stands right now. I can't think of a better golf course for those who really like to think through their shots, nor one that is a sterner examination of grace under fire. Let the emotions get the better of you, and you're finished."

A rough decision

Ultimately, the USGA's decisions on course conditions were predicated in part on two dry runs. The Open would be the culmination of an exhausting 10 months at Pebble Beach, as the course hosted the U.S. Amateur in August 1999, and the AT&T Pro-Am in February 2000. The USGA was in the unique position of determining a year in advance the conditions it would like, then watching some of the world's top golfers play in that environment to see if it would bear fruit.

For example, Tom Meeks, the USGA's head of competition, determined the five-plus inches to which the rough grew at the Amateur was far too penal. Thus, the USGA planned to have the main rough just a shade over three inches for the Open. The idea was to give players an opportunity to play forward, with varying levels of risk. Similar conditions had been established the previous year at Pinehurst No. 2 in North Carolina. The result was that Payne Stewart won the championship with an overall score of even-par.

"We're all the same out of five and six inches of

rough," said Paul Azinger, who won the 1991 AT&T Pro-Am at Pebble Beach. He liked the idea of players needing to control a hot shot out of the deep rough onto a rock-hard green. "I think there is a great art lost and a great skill lost when we don't have the opportunity to hit fliers. There's nothing more challenging than playing a flier to a hard green."

"There's an old Scottish saying that 'If there's nae wind, there's nae gowf,' and it's a sentiment with which I heartily concur."

— Jack Nicklaus

Having given the players a chance to gamble from the rough, the USGA decided to up the ante as the Open approached. The decision was made by Meeks and Tim Moraghan, lead agronomist for the USGA, to grow the rough to four inches.

"At three, three and a half inches, it didn't bring out the half-shot penalty we like to have occur," Moraghan said.

What the USGA didn't want to see, for example, was players driving into the right rough on the par-5 sixth hole, then still reaching the green in two. In other words, they did not want the rough to be a hedge against aggressive play.

The change was met with mixed reactions. "I cannot hit it out of the rough on this golf course, unless I get lucky," said Watson, an expert on the subject in that his chip from the rough on No. 17 clinched a win at the 1982 Open. "For me, it's impossible."

The USGA determined that Pebble's uniformly tiny greens presented challenge enough by way of shape and texture. Without any changes, a sufficient premium would be placed on a golfer's ability to play target golf, especially given the slender fairways averaging just 30 yards in width. The greens would, however, be slick at 11.5 on the stimpmeter.

Phil Mickelson, winner of the 1998 AT&T Pro-Am, predicted that 288 — 8-over par — would win the championship.

"It's almost impossible to make birdies, the greens are so hard," Mickelson said.

Tiger Woods concurred.

"You feel like you might want to leave the putter cover on," Woods said. "The greens are totally unforgiving in every sense."

While Meeks said he was willing to "tweak" the course a bit during the week, he said he would not watch the scoreboard to help him decide whether or

Pebble Beach grounds crew members mow the fourth fairway against a backdrop of Stillwater Cove.

The U.S. Open Village — A City Within a City

In their effort to stage an event in keeping with the grandeur of the 100th U.S. Open, championship organizers at Pebble Beach needed more room.

The inherent difficulty in housing a massive event at Pebble Beach is that fans can only stand on one side of the fairway. The ocean, you see, long ago laid claim to the other side.

"The challenge was to enlarge the acreage that we had," championship director RJ Harper said. "But the golf course is what it is."

Organizers couldn't just tear up a few holes on the golf course, could they?

Well, yes they could, Harper told them — but it would be the par-3 Peter Hay Golf Course alongside Pebble Beach.

The warm-up and practice course sits on five acres just up the hill from Pebble Beach's first tee. During the three previous U.S. Opens at Pebble Beach, the site had been used to park service trailers and house behind-the-scenes facilities. But Harper proposed that Peter Hay be razed so the main merchandise tent and spectator village could be built there — leaving more room on the main golf course.

The U.S. Open Village would also boast a championship museum and Payne's Place, a pub in which patrons could inscribe in a book fond memories of the place's namesake, late Open champion Payne Stewart.

To boot, the village included one of the most spectacular entrances ever seen at a major sporting event, replete with marble columns and a 15-foot bronze monument sculpted by one of America's greatest living artisans, Richard MacDonald.

"From the moment they walked onto the grounds, we wanted people to know they were attending an event unlike any they'd ever been to," Harper said.

The creation of the U.S. Open Village would make a lot of things possible for the Pebble Beach championship organizers, who sold 35,000 tickets to the event per day — 10,000 more than when the Open was held at Pebble in 1992.

Thus, the bulldozers uprooted six holes at Peter Hay, leaving the remaining holes intact to create a relaxed park-like setting. Ultimately, the little course played a big part in presenting the big show.

not to alter conditions.

"We're not going to let the scores change our strategy," Meeks said.

Second opinion

Why?

That was first thing that crossed most players' minds as they walked up to the second tee and saw the sign: "Hole 2, Par-4, 484 yards."

The reasoning was complicated — and ironic, as the USGA, which typically holds golf's history as sacred, thumbed its nose at tradition for the 2000 Open.

In the three previous Open championships at Pebble Beach, the second hole played as a 506-yard par 5. Now the course would go from having been a 6,840-yard par 72 to a par 71 of approximately the same length. The second hole was rarely a difficult test of par — playing to a course-low stroke average of 4.86 at the Open in 1972, 4.69 in 1982, and 4.65 in 1992. But No. 2 stood the test of time, which to purists was value enough.

"Why change something that you have a historical reference to?" asked Tiger Woods. "We've always played this course as a par 72 — the major championships, the AT&T, the Crosbys. All of a sudden, we make it a par-71. I don't think it's right."

Woods wasn't alone in his thinking.

"I don't think it's a good idea," said 2000 Masters champion Vijay Singh, "because the golf course was set up to be a par 5. That's the strength of the whole course — you have a good start and you face those hard holes coming in."

The change was put into motion in 1998, when the Monterey pine that for decades stood guard at the left-center entrance to the green lost its battle to Pitch Canker — a unique botanical disease threatening pines on the Monterey Peninsula. For the 1999 U.S. Amateur Championship, the USGA made its move, setting up the hole as a par 4 at 484 yards. Officials found that most players were able to hit 4-irons or 5-irons into the green.

Players remained nonplussed. "The green on No. 2 is not designed to accept long irons. It's not a green for a par 4," Singh said.

The move to a par 4 was not without its supporters, however. The change was appropriate and inevitable, according to 1992 champion Tom Kite.

"The so-called stand between par 4 and par 5 is going out the window," said Kite, who also won the 1983 Pro-Am at Pebble Beach. "The golf ball is going further. The lightweight metal woods and the conditioning of the players are allowing the guys to get it so much further than before. Guys regularly drive the ball 280, 300 yards — and not even the big guys."

The U.S. Open Monument

One morning, as the early arrivals at the 100th U.S. Open came to watch practice rounds, a man stopped to admire the 15-foot-tall golf sculpture that stood as the centerpiece to the spectators' village at Pebble Beach.

"I never expected anything like this," he said, gripped by the towering bronze monument that stood on a granite base.

It was just what Richard MacDonald wanted to hear. Standing nearby, the artist who created the piece knew he had achieved his goal: a distinguished legacy to the game. Titled "A Monument for the 100th U.S. Open: Encircling Centuries of Excellence," the striking bronze depiction of the golf swing was unveiled at Pebble Beach during a private ceremony on June 2, two weeks before the competition began. But it was 10,000 hours in the making that started when MacDonald, an internationally acclaimed sculptor who lives in Monterey, agreed a year before to collaborate on the monument with the Pebble Beach Company.

The result of MacDonald's meticulousness is a figure that captures the powerful movement of the golf swing, as well as its grace and fluidity — not surprising, considering MacDonald used professional golfers as models. MacDonald's golfer remains true to detail, from the overlap grip to the creases in his slacks, while leaving room to imagine the shot exploding off a club that is so subtly worked into the monument that it almost goes unnoticed. And it is immovable — which is ironic, because the sculpture itself appears to be moving when viewed. In fact, the monument will be a permanent fixture at Pebble Beach, and will bear the names of U.S. Open winners in perpetuity.

Top photo: *Volunteers gather at Robert Louis Stevenson School to make plaid ribbons commemorating defending champion Payne Stewart. The ribbons sold for $1 and the proceeds benefited the Payne Stewart Foundation.*

Above: *The ribbons were worn by all championship officials and volunteers.*

Next page: *A pub — dubbed Payne's Place — offered a place for patrons to relax in the U.S. Open Village and watch a big-screen telecast or sign a book in memory of the place's namesake.*

Moving the fifth

While the debate over the change on No. 2 continued, nobody fussed over Pebble Beach's new fifth hole — a 188-yard par 3 rebuilt in 1998 by Jack Nicklaus to run along Stillwater Cove, giving the course eight contiguous oceanside holes. The new hole replaced a nondescript one that ran uphill, creating a blind shot to the green.

The obvious difference in the approach to the new hole was the exposure to the ocean winds. It took Nicklaus, himself, five shots to finally stick the green in a casual round with friend Andy Bean prior to the Open.

Nicklaus didn't agree, however, with the USGA growing thick rough along the left side so close to the green. "They're not going to play it the way we designed it," he said. "It's supposed to be fairway there, so you can feed the ball to the green."

Nicklaus predicted the hole would play tougher than the players might expect. It ranked fourth in difficulty during the 2000 AT&T Pro-Am, with a scoring average of 3.21.

"There's nowhere to bail out," said two-time U.S. Open champion Lee Janzen. "You either have to hit the green or do something miraculous to make par."

CHAPTER FOUR

The World Watches

With golf more popular than ever, a record number of media were to descend to chronicle the centennial Open.

Beach Club members look out over Stillwater Cove and the pier that became home to an ESPN booth during the championship.

Photographers have their eyes (and their lenses) on the prize.

Record numbers

Just below the east end of the Pebble Beach polo field, a grassy clearing edged by aging Monterey pines is nicknamed "The Beetle Farm." During the annual AT&T Pebble Beach National Pro-Am, it serves as headquarters for an army of volunteer marshals.

For the 100th U.S. Open, however, it would be the locale for a media colossus designed to meet the demand for information resulting from golf's ever-expanding popularity.

While the 2000 championship drew a record 8,457 player entries and the event was a sellout for a record 14th straight year, the media was also expected to come in huge numbers — close to 2,000 altogether. The number of scribes on site would reflect golf's millennial renaissance, and make the 100th U.S. Open the most heavily covered golf tournament of all time.

The media compound, spanning four acres and operated by the communications staff of the United States Golf Association, was designed to house the record number of writers, photographers, television and radio personnel for the week. From Glasgow to Greensboro, Tokyo to San Diego, media would come from 25 countries around the world, as well as Jupiter (Florida, that is). Television networks NBC and ESPN planned an unmatched 28 hours of combined live coverage.

Inside the media center's tented boundaries, nearly 1,000 yards of identical work stations ran parallel to one another, awaiting some of the world's most elite chroniclers of sport and society. Belying the center's spartan and antiseptic nature, within its confines would stand some of the most inventive and colorful minds to cover the game. It would be a place where veteran writers Furman Bisher, James Dodson and Dan Jenkins would sit side-by-side with more *avante garde* scribes like *Sports Illustrated's* Rick Reilly and the *Los Angeles Times'* Thomas Bonk. Likewise, television personalities like ESPN's Chris Berman and CNN's Jim Huber would greet the masses alongside burgeoning Internet personalities like Helen Ross and Mark Soltau.

Doing justice

Tom Roy, NBC's executive producer of the network's golf team, came into the event with a

heightened understanding of the significance of the event and its venue.

"I'm more excited about this Open than any other I've ever done," said Roy, who has been involved in golf telecasts since 1984. "With the historical nature of it being the 100th U.S. Open, it's going to be the benchmark event in American golf."

Roy was also excited about the new technology NBC would employ in its U.S. Open coverage. The network was to unveil its "boat-cam," a camera on a boat that zoomed in on play along Pebble Beach's oceanside holes. It was the same technology NBC used in its coverage of America's Cup sailing. Also, NBC would use global positioning satellites to provide detailed on-course statistical information.

"Broadcasters who have done events there have done a terrific job of showing the beauty of the place," Roy said, referring to CBS's annual coverage of the AT&T Pro-Am. "But the first time I played there, I was surprised at how good each and every hole is — not only beautiful, but a great golf hole. We really made a huge effort to pick camera locations to show how good the holes are, how wonderful this place is."

Previous page top photo: *NBC analyst Roger Maltbie gets his makeup touched up prior to filming a U.S. Open preview show.*

Previous page bottom photo: *The U.S. Open trophy sits on the NBC set, ready for its close-up.*

Left: *Maltbie jokes with Jack Nicklaus as Nicklaus completes the 10th hole behind the NBC set.*

Bottom: *Thousands of members of the print media would fill the media center to chronicle the Open.*

Following page: *NBC color analyst Johnny Miller has brought unabashed commentary to the game of golf.*

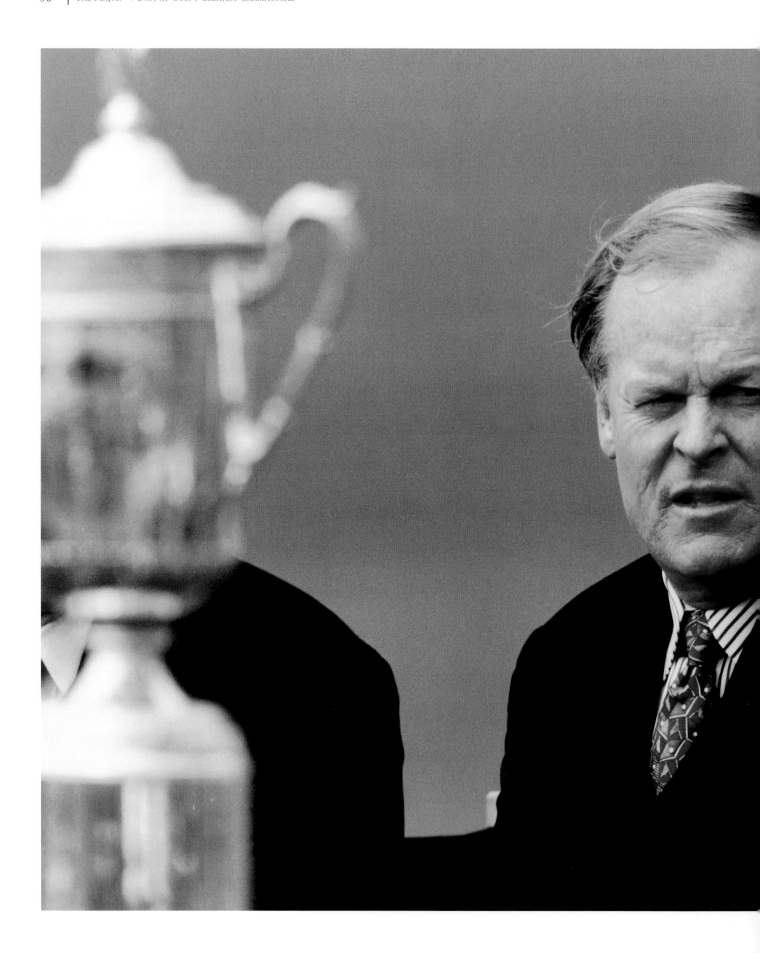

Johnny Miller

It all happened so spontaneously, the first time neophyte NBC color analyst Johnny Miller mentioned "choking" on the air.

During the final round of the 1990 Bob Hope Chrysler Classic, as leader Peter Jacobsen was about to hit from a downhill lie in the fairway, with a carry over water 220 yards to the green, Miller offered this analysis: "You know, this is the perfect time for him to choke on it."

If you were a viewer accustomed to the reverent hushes of most golf announcers, you were astonished that Miller would be so cavalier as to say "choke" on the air, but impressed that he was absolutely right — Jacobsen, as if on cue, plopped his shot in the water.

In his debut as a television commentator, Miller, a man whose 24 Tour wins were highlighted by victories at the 1973 U.S. Open and the 1976 British Open, was instantly beloved by viewers, yet vilified by the players with whom he was once aligned. At that moment, Johnny Miller became both the voice of reason, and the voice of treason.

Miller was never more audacious than at the 1999 Ryder Cup at The Country Club in Brookline, MA. He referred to prohibitive favorite Jim Furyk as an "underdog" in his match against teenager Sergio Garcia, and suggested that American Justin Leonard, winless in seven Ryder Cup matches, stay home and watch Saturday afternoon play on television. When Leonard's 45-foot birdie putt clinched an improbable come-from-behind victory for the United States, Miller referred to the ensuing on-course celebration as an "embarrassment."

"I actually changed the way golf was announced," said Miller, who won three Crosby/AT&T Pro-Ams at Pebble Beach, as well as a State Amateur championship there in 1968. "I'm not saying I'm the World Wrestling Federation, but golf was getting to the point where it needed to move to a new level, more mainstream. It was ready for more pointed commentary and more honesty."

Miller promised the same unbridled commentary during his stay at the 100th U.S. Open.

"To me, behavior is the most interesting thing in the game of golf," said Miller, 53, a Pebble Beach neighbor by way of his home in nearby Pacific Grove. "For all those years (as a player), I was mesmerized by how people acted under pressure. I didn't know I was going to be an announcer, but it was like I was doing my doctorate thesis on choking."

CHAPTER FIVE

The Powers That Be

The 100th Open would be a coming out party for a star-studded Pebble Beach ownership.

Right: *Pebble Beach co-owner Clint Eastwood, Minnesota governor Jesse Ventura and former White House Chief of Staff Leon Panetta were among the big names on hand at Pebble Beach for the centennial celebration.*

Below: *Eastwood and Ventura are among the few who have used their celebrity to gain public office, Ventura as Minnesota's pro-wrestler-turned-governor and movie star Eastwood in becoming the mayor of Carmel.*

Next page: *Arnold Palmer gives Jack Nicklaus a thumbs-up as the Golden Bear plays Pebble Beach's second hole during a weekend practice round.*

The art of the deal

Exactly one year prior to the start of the 100th U.S. Open, the price of paradise was revealed.

Emerging from Pebble Beach's Club XIX, Peter Ueberroth and Dick Ferris confirmed they and principal partners Clint Eastwood and Arnold Palmer had reached an agreement to buy the Pebble Beach Company from the Japanese-owned Lone Cypress Company for $820 million.

The star-studded ownership, along with approximately 100 high-profile investors, would take control of the prestigious U.S. Open venue, three other golf courses and two luxury hotels. Moreover, it was an opportunity to replant the American flag in an iconic sporting venue that had been under foreign ownership since 1990.

"I can't think of a happier time," said Ferris, who formerly helmed both United Airlines and Hertz Rent-A-Car, and was now the head of the PGA Tour Policy Board. "I look at this as a stewardship for years ahead, and being with good friends and associates in doing it."

The agreement was the realization of a vision that Ueberroth and Ferris, close friends since 1961, shared as much as six years prior.

"We began thinking, 'Wouldn't it be great to have a whole bunch of people own this property in perpetuity?'" said Ueberroth, the former Commissioner of Baseball and Olympic Committee chairman who was *Time's* Man of the Year in 1984.

It was the goal of the new group to put a stop to the seemingly constant buying and selling of Pebble Beach. *Golf Digest* wrote that Pebble Beach was "the land that humbled a billionaire, bankrupted a Japanese boom-time golden boy, and, most recently, sent an army of Japanese bankers back home with little to show for their seven years of superlative stewardship."

Pebble Beach's buy-and-sell gauntlet began in 1978, when 20th Century Fox purchased Pebble Beach for $72 million. But three years after buying Pebble, Fox was sold for approximately $722 million in a deal that included the movie studio's various other holdings, including Aspen ski resort and the famous golf links.

Enter a new owner, Marvin Davis, a man known as "Mr. Wildcatter" for the windfall he made in Colorado oil.

"I'm a golfer," Davis told *Golf Digest*. "And Pebble Beach was *it*."

Previous page: *Jack Nicklaus, the designer of Pebble Beach's fifth hole and numerous other course modifications, tees off on the ninth hole during a weekend practice round.*

Top: *Two Pebble Beach employees prepare for the dedication of the new fifth hole at Pebble Beach.*

Above: *New Pebble Beach owners Clint Eastwood, Richard Ferris, Arnold Palmer, and Peter Ueberroth presented a plaque to the company's former Japanese ownership, congratulating them on their foresight in acquiring the land that became the course's new fifth hole.*

Despite selling off his other Fox assets, Davis invested heavily in the Pebble Beach Company, building the coastal Links at Spanish Bay along with making numerous other capital improvements.

"I hadn't planned on selling," Davis said. "But the price got so high..."

Minoru Isutani was the outrageous captain of Japanese golf in the 1980s, building a number of private golf courses and selling $25,000 gold-plated golf clubs.

Isutani coveted Pebble Beach, and offered to purchase it for approximately $850 million, more than $700 million above its estimated value. "We shook hands on it, and that was it," Davis said.

Isutani instantly drew the ire of locals when it was divulged he planned to sell 1,000 memberships to Pebble Beach at $1 million each, allowing members to reserve tee times years in advance, and leaving a scant few daily spots for nonmembers.

Isutani's plan was blocked by the California Coastal Commission. Sumitomo Bank attempted to refinance his loan the same week Isutani's company filed for bankruptcy. After less than two years of ownership, Isutani sold Pebble Beach in 1992 to an amalgam of Sumitomo and Taiheiyo Club Inc., operator of a large number of golf courses in Japan,

Nicklaus opens Pasadera Country Club

Jack Nicklaus has never been the type to ask for a free ride. Hard work has always been his answer to achieving goals, whether he was climbing the ranks as a young player or building his highly successful Golden Bear International.

June 11, 2000, marked another milestone for Nicklaus: the formal opening of Pasadera Country Club, the first course of his own design on the Monterey Peninsula. While his championships at Pebble Beach are part of his legend — the U.S. Amateur in 1961, his U.S. Open triumph in 1972, and his three victories in the annual Pro-Am — Pasadera was both his business and his pleasure to build, given his passion for the area that many deem the world's golf kingdom.

It is often the case in life that as one door closes, another opens. So it would be for Nicklaus, as Pasadera's unveiling dovetailed with the playing of his 44th and final U.S. Open.

"Pasadera represents a watershed moment for me, to be sure," said Nicklaus, who made frequent trips to the West Coast to supervise Pasadera's three-year construction. "One of my greatest accomplishments was to become part of the fabric of a place like the Monterey Peninsula. Now I'm leaving my imprint in a real, permanent way. I'd say it's a major point of pride, and it represents a nice transition in my life."

Pasadera, a gated, custom-home community located in the hills above the famous Laguna Seca Racetrack, has as its centerpiece a soaring 6,811-yard, par-71 championship golf course. Bathed in sunshine, the opulent course is threaded by a thoroughfare called "Oso D'Oro Court" — Spanish for Golden Bear Court.

In fact, Pasadera represented a seminal accomplishment for Nicklaus, 60, as he transitioned from Golden Bear to Greying Bear.

"I worked pretty hard this spring to get my golf game somewhat respectable," said Nicklaus, who had his hip replaced midway through Pasadera's construction. "I was respectable for a couple of rounds at Augusta (in April 2000), and fell on my face, you might say, the last two rounds. I'd like to not have that happen at the Open. I'd like to play reasonably respectable golf.

"But I've worked hard at the darned game for 40 years — almost 40 years of professional golf. And, frankly, I'm tired of that."

These days, Nicklaus said his greatest satisfaction comes from the involvement of his four sons — Jack II, Steve, Mike and Gary — in the design business. In fact, Jack II contributed heavily to Pasadera's construction.

"I take great pride in knowing that one of my legacies will be the mark my whole family is making as golf course designers," Nicklaus said. "They've taken my philosophies and added their own personal touches."

The boys said their dad is still as competitive in the design business as he was on the golf course. "When he makes up his mind, that's it," Steve said. "You're not going to change his mind."

As he prepared to leave the game he helped define, Nicklaus suggested that projects like Pasadera are representative of the serenity he finally found away from golf.

"I've played my golf," he said. "That doesn't mean I don't want to play anymore. But life is more than just playing a silly game."

The sixth, seventh, and eighth holes of the Pebble Beach Golf Links are located on one of the most scenic stretches of land in the world.

The seawall along the left of Pebble Beach's famed 18th hole is all that stands between the fairway and the Pacific. Taiheiyo Club Inc. modified the wall as one of its numerous capital improvements before selling the property in 1999.

for $500 million. The new owners promised to "polish the jewel of California."

The new owners built the new Spa at Pebble Beach and Casa Palmero, a new luxury hotel. They installed a new seawall along the 18th fairway, and purchased the seaside land necessary to build a spectacular new fifth hole. However, Taiheiyo was brought to its knees in 1998 by its own financiers. In Japan, banks began seeking salable assets, as private funds were being used to bail out the country's plunging banking industry.

Taiheiyo's goal was to return Pebble Beach to the best possible American ownership, one that would purchase the property without an exit strategy. Taiheiyo did not want to sell at such a high price as to sentence the new owner to a cumbersome debt service, thereby perpetuating the cycle of buy-and-sell at Pebble Beach.

Taiheiyo decided to entertain four suitors, including Ueberroth's Contrarian Group, which helped convert Doubletree Hotels from a company with 15 properties to one with 1,400 hotels and billions of dollars in assets. Ueberroth saw opportunity in Pebble Beach, which he deemed to be an underutilized asset in terms

of capitalizing on the place's name recognition. But he and Ferris, who Ueberroth referred to as "the best hotel man in the world," had to assemble an ownership group with integrity that would make them the best possible successor to Taiheiyo.

Putting the group together

Ueberroth immediately contacted Bill Perocchi, 38, a rising star in the hotel industry who increased Promus Hotel Corp.'s assets from $250 million to $4 billion. Ueberroth and Ferris held a large number of shares in Promus, and wanted Perocchi to head the day-to-day operations at Pebble Beach, were the purchase to go through.

Ferris then reached Palmer, who he had come to know when Palmer was a pitchman for Hertz. Ueberroth contacted his golfing buddy Eastwood, well-known on the Monterey Peninsula not only for his films but for having been the mayor of Carmel. The two also served together on the Monterey Peninsula Golf Foundation, which operates the AT&T Pebble Beach National Pro-Am, and Eastwood was the new owner of Tehama Golf Club above Carmel Valley.

A golfer rips his second shot up 50 feet of elevated, sun-baked fairway during a weekend round.

A foursome finishes up on Pebble Beach's shortest hole, No. 7, as yachts and fishing boats pass by.

"We needed someone of great local stature, which is what Clint brought to our group," Ueberroth said. "Arnold is a great guy for Pebble's golf people to turn and talk to. Dick (Ferris) is a Cornell University hotel school graduate and spent most of his career in the resort business. I was in the mix just in case they built a Little League field in back somewhere."

The four partners split up approximately $100 million of the $820 million asking price, and added GE Pension Fund as a primary financier. Ueberroth then came up with the idea to mix in an elite list of minority partners with an ability to purchase $2 million shares.

"If you had enough investors so there would be no one dominant — no Marvin Davis who could sell it — that would work," Ueberroth said. "And it did."

In June 1999, some of America's richest golfers received a prospectus on the deal. Within two months, approximately 100 investors had signed up, including NFL star John Elway and Charles Schwab.

Positioned for growth

With a calendar year standing between them and the U.S. Open, the new group's challenge was to put in place a business system that would preserve the property, all the while preparing Pebble Beach as the venue for the U.S. Open.

The owners encouraged U.S. Open organizers to forget everything that had ever been done at previous major events at Pebble Beach and to focus on presenting an event like none other.

"We had to start from scratch and create a fresh palette from which to paint," said RJ Harper, the Open's championship director.

Tour guides were to be placed on each shuttle bus to welcome spectators and provide information during the ride from their cars to the course. The par-3 Peter Hay Golf Course alongside Pebble Beach was to be converted into a gorgeous U.S. Open Village. Massive grandstands with theater-style seats were to be assembled around the course to give the event a sense of grandeur. Nine hospitality tents were to be built along the hillside above the sixth fairway with a view of Stillwater Cove.

"We want the U.S. Open to be a standard-bearer for our company," Ueberroth said. "Arnold Palmer told our people, 'Let's make this the greatest major championship ever — nothing less.' I think that the work everyone has done on this has put us in a position to do just that."

Crew cut

The other man's grass is always greener — unless, of course, you happen to be the other man.

Eric Greytok is the 27-year-old superintendent of golf — the guy in charge of the grass, so to speak — at Pebble Beach, which is something like being in charge of the weather in heaven. Ryan Wyckoff, only 25, and Jack Holt, a 19-year fixture at the golf links, are his first lieutenants.

Their task: make the world's greatest golf course perfect. Or better.

Never was that challenge more daunting than in the weeks preceding the 100th U.S. Open, when the three men and their crew of 25 groundskeepers groomed Pebble Beach for what was arguably the most important event in the course's history. For Pebble's supers, this was the Super Bowl.

"The U.S. Open has given us all something to shoot for. It's given us a goal," Wyckoff said. "It tends to light that spark again and get you focused."

They watched the sun rise each morning over Stillwater Cove, and saw it set most nights. In between, Greytok and crew groomed Pebble's 100 acres of emerald turf, trimming it daily with four greens mowers, four tees-and-approaches mowers, four fairway mowers, and two more for the rough.

Mark Thomas, Pebble's veteran irrigation technician, utilized an elaborate computer system to bathe the course in 100,000 to 500,000 gallons of water, depending on the weather. Rick Pieper, the spray tech since 1977, wandered the grounds relentlessly with his nutrients and fertilizers. Greytok, who apprenticed at Congressional Country Club in Bethesda, MD, and Merion (PA) Golf Club before coming to Pebble, walked the course once each morning, and again every afternoon, checking the smallest details and making notes.

His platoon toted hoses, shovels, and rakes through the morning fog and afternoon sunshine. They raked the bunkers, repaired ball marks, filled divots, whacked weeds, hand-watered dry spots, and appeared to enjoy every chore. "Not a bad place to come to work every morning," said Wyckoff, smiling contentedly at the understatement.

CHAPTER SIX

A Foreign Affair

As Open week began, a new generation of foreign players expressed a strong desire to calm 30 years of stormy seas.

Above: *Vijay Singh and Greg Norman share a laugh during a Monday practice round.*

Nick Faldo tees off during a Monday practice round he hoped would help him regain the form that led to six major titles.

A singular cause

With Irish brogue and English lilt, they took Johnny Miller's name in vain.

There sat European golf's new guard — Darren Clarke, Lee Westwood, and Thomas Bjorn — stolen away to the rear of Pebble Beach's Tap Room at the outset of U.S. Open week. Around the table, they looked like a conceptual drawing of a place where the heather grows long and the beer flows smooth after midnight mass. They were stock-thick, iron-armed cats with eyes so wet you'd swear they just turned away from the teeth of a north wind.

To a man, they were incensed by Miller's comments on a U.S. Open preview show. The NBC commentator said the reason that only one European had won the U.S. Open since 1927 was because they were intimidated to be standing in tall Yankee grass. Hearing this, European sports agent Chubby Chandler gathered clients Clarke and Westwood to discuss rallying the boys from the other side of the Atlantic.

"Pathetic, absolutely pathetic," Chandler said of Miller's comments. "The man was very close to sounding like an idiot."

Within hours, word had spread to the other 10

Nineteen-year-old Aussie wunderkind Aaron Baddeley plays alongside his idol Greg Norman, whom he beat in the Australian Open to earn his exemption for the 100th U.S. Open.

The Jack Nicklaus-designed fifth hole, which opened for play in January 1999, sits upon the bluffs above Stillwater Cove as fans gather to watch a Monday practice round.

Lee Westwood walks up the 14th green, which slopes severely back toward the fairway, making the par-5 the toughest hole on the Links. Westwood was among several European Ryder Cup players who bristled at the thought of being intimidated by American conditions.

Match-play champion Darren Clarke takes a break during a Monday practice round to oblige autograph seekers.

European players in the Open field. Now they stood with one mission: To take the pages of the U.S. Open's history book — yellow, frayed, and covered with a century's dust — and scatter them into the Pacific winds.

Long odds

The Europeans had dominated the Ryder Cup over the previous two decades. At Augusta National, the Green Jacket had adorned the shoulders of six European Masters champions in the previous 10 years. But for Europeans at the American national championship, the U.S. Open cup had been as dry as Beefeater gin.

The last European player to take the Open title was England's Tony Jacklin in 1970. Jacklin, 25 at the time, stopped another serious drought, as he was the first British player to win the U.S. Open since Cyril Walker in 1924. Competing at Hazeltine National Golf Club in winds as strong as 40 mph, Jacklin buckled down to crush runner-up Dave Hill by seven strokes.

The victories by Jacklin and Walker stand out among a sparse few moments of European glory at the U.S.

Open, along with wins by Edward Ray in 1920, James Barnes in 1921, and Scotland's William McFarland in 1925 and Tommy Armour in 1927. In fact, only four non-Americans — Jacklin, Gary Player, David Graham, and Ernie Els — had won the American national championship in the past 68 years.

Rough times

According to most European players, the culprit in their U.S. Open futility was the heavy rough employed by the United States Golf Association in championship course layouts.

"Understand this: We don't grow long grass on our courses," Chandler said. "In the past the top Europeans played only at home, and their games reflected it. That's why Seve Ballesteros could never win the U.S. Open."

Sweden's Jesper Parnevik echoed the sentiment.

"A lot of the guys just aren't familiar with the courses here," Parnevik said. "Plus, we're not used to playing in high rough and tight fairways."

The Europeans' experience at the 2000 Masters bore this out. Augusta National officials decided to grow

Bob May, who has enjoyed greater success in Europe than in the States, hits an approach shot to the 10th green with grandstands and the "Cliffs of Doom" in the background.

the rough at the 2000 tournament to 1.5 inches — meager compared to the 4-inch rough they'd confront at Pebble Beach. Consequently, the best finish by a European player was 19th place, by Colin Montgomerie and Frenchman Jean Van de Velde.

Indeed, Europeans are used to courses designed by Mother Nature and tended by Father Time. In Europe, tournament conditions are generally the product of evolution rather than manipulation. There, tradition is such that tournament officials take great care not to alter what their forefathers intended.

> *"Understand this: We don't grow long grass on our courses. In the past the top Europeans played only at home, and their games reflected it. That's why Seve Ballesteros could never win the U.S. Open."*
>
> — European agent Chubby Chandler

"Almost unilaterally, the only defenses European courses have are rock-hard fairways and wind," said Peter Thomson, who won five British Open titles on different venues, including St. Andrews in 1956. "Where to hit? You can't aim down the treeline because there are no trees. Rough line? There's no rough to speak of. Aim at the bunkers? Sure, though much of the time you can't see them.

"In Europe, you expect to play around the deep pot bunkers, and have greens with undulations that easily roll approaches far off line. That forces players to lag 100-foot putts. None of those skills come into play in America."

While Pebble Beach elicits more passion than any other golf course stateside, such was not the case among the Europeans.

"I'd prefer to play elsewhere," Westwood said. "The course isn't in my Top 10."

"In America?" he was asked.

"In California," Westwood replied.

A new attitude

By the Monday prior to the 100th Open, it was evident that the Europeans felt poised for a revival as they strode across Pebble Beach during their practice rounds. With the usual cast of veterans there in force, the European roster was deepened by young talent like Spain's Sergio Garcia, 20, Sweden's Bjorn, 29, Ireland's Padraig Harrington, 28, and late-blooming Miguel Angel Jimenez, 36.

Former British Open champion Greg Norman chips onto the third green during a Monday practice round.

"It's getting where the young guys have been here a couple times, and they're getting used to playing in this championship," Bjorn said. "Now we know what we're getting into. It takes a while to understand what it's all about. I think that's why you see more Europeans on the leaderboard and why I think you'll see even more in the future."

Indeed, the image of the European player scrambling from the gorse to save par seemed to be evolving to comply with the American game.

"Monty and Darren are the two most impressive ball strikers in the world," Tiger Woods said. "And Jimenez is one of the great drivers of the ball in golf. I wouldn't be surprised to see any of them high on the leaderboard."

Van de Velde's comments as he left the course were pointed directly toward a seismic change in the Europeans' fate.

"You can rewrite history as you wish," he said. "That's life, you know. Get a handkerchief and cry someplace else. It's a new era. Let's see how Johnny Miller likes that."

Opposite page: *Longtime swing coach Butch Harmon works with Tiger Woods at the driving range.*

Above: *Coach Steve Mata drills with Vijay Singh.*

Right: *Embattled golfer John Daly, who withdrew from the 1999 U.S. Open at Pinehurst, hoped a new approach would work in 2000.*

Home on the Range

One particular section of grandstand seats filled early in the morning and emptied late in the afternoon every day during the U.S. Open. The prized ducats weren't even for the golf course. Rather, they were for the driving range.

For the same reason baseball fans flock to the ballpark to watch Mark McGwire and Sammy Sosa take batting practice, true golf aficionados hit the range to see Tiger Woods and John Daly hit 200-yard shots with their 7-irons, and stood close enough to hear the startled hiss of the ball leaving their drivers.

The Pebble Beach range was reincarnated from an unassuming warm-up area into a first-class contestant compound, complete with a two-story tent that served as the players' private clubhouse for the week. The range provided more than pure entertainment; it was an outdoor classroom where the ticket-holding public got an education as to how the game's greatest craftsmen go about fine-tuning their art.

Fans watched David Duval and Ernie Els polish their mid-iron games, shaping shot after shot against the backdrop of the thick Del Monte Forest. They also observed the hundreds of sand shots a short-game perfectionist like Lee Janzen hits from a buried lie late in the afternoon.

Conspicuous were the swing coaches, who were increasingly becoming fixtures on Tour. Butch Harmon was there with prize pupil Woods, and longtime teacher Jim Flick was on hand to check on student Jack Nicklaus. Virtually every player was joined by a mentor at one point or another.

Fans were privy to the commercial side of the game as well. One might have observed Vijay Singh return a bag of balls to the range attendant because they were not Titleists, the balls he's contracted to play.

"In 1992, we charged players money for the balls," tournament director RJ Harper said. "Suffice it to say, things have changed. The players keep our guys bouncing."

Patrons of Stillwater Village, a cluster of lavish corporate tents along the third fairway, likely came to the Open feeling they'd have the best seats in the house. Though less ornate, the golf junkie sitting a chip shot away from the game's great practitioners might have presented a good argument.

CHAPTER SEVEN

A Truly Open Open

*For every superstar, there was a
wide-eyed qualifier landing at Pebble Beach
who proved the Open is sports' great democracy.*

As a teenager in Carmel Valley, Bobby Clampett used to sneak onto the Pebble Beach course to play. After winning two state championships at Pebble Beach, as well as finishing third at the 1992 U.S. Open, his career went into a mysterious decline. He retired in 1995, and had played in just one tournament in two years leading up to the U.S. Open.

CBS announcer Bobby Clampett emerged from being an unlikely fourth alternate in sectional qualifying to earning a spot at Pebble Beach, just a block away from where he attended high school.

The great democracy

The word no one pays much attention to is "Open."

In the end, the 2000 U.S. Open championship, like all major golf tournaments, would likely belong to a highly skilled and dedicated 52-weeks-a-year member of the PGA or European Tour. But on Day 1, the most eyebrow-raising story inevitably comes from one of the improbables — a could've-been or never-was who dared go through regional or sectional qualifying to become one of the U.S. Open's 156 participants. While 70 of the field's entrants gained exemptions based on past accomplishments, the other 86 rose from a record 8,457 golfers with 1.4-handicap indexes or lower who vied for an Open slot in 2000.

Life is made of dreams, and Bobby Clampett's dream made for the most compelling story at the 2000 Open.

While some were established Tour players past and present, many were hoboes and hopefuls, migrants following the golf harvest. The majority of the year they play on foggy Mondays, on tours where no ropes are necessary to contain the fans, and every day is sudden death.

Now they'd found themselves at the rainbow's end — Pebble Beach — where the steaks are two inches thick and the wind blows like perfume.

Patron saints

Each of the long shots arrived on the Monterey Peninsula taking solace in the three patron saints of Open qualifying — Francis Ouimet, Jack Fleck, and Steve Jones.

In 1913, Ouimet, a 20-year-old amateur who lived across the street from The Country Club in Brookline, MA, stunned English greats Harry Vardon and Ted Ray in a play-off. Ouimet became the only golfer to win the first Open in which he played.

In 1955, Ben Hogan was all but assured of his record fifth Open title until Fleck had the audacity to play the

David Duval and Shigeki Maruyama wait on the 10th tee. Maruyama shot a 58 in Open qualifying.

last four holes in 2-under par to force a playoff. At the time, Hogan had 62 Tour wins and Fleck none, but the underdog shocked the world, prevailing by three strokes on the extra 18 at Olympic Club.

Jones, who had grown up playing sand greens in Eastern Colorado, stunned Davis Love III and Tom Lehman at Oakland Hills in 1996. The victory came two years to the day after Jones was severely injured in a motorcycle accident and nearly retired.

Dream of dreams

Life is made of dreams. Bobby Clampett believes this to his core. And with all due respect to Shigeki Maruyama, the 30-year-old Japanese Tour pro who shot a 58 in sectional qualifying at Woodmont C.C. in Rockville, Md., Clampett's story was the most endearing at the 2000 Open.

Clampett, who was born and raised in nearby Carmel Valley, would be the championship's native son. A one-time prodigy of Tiger Woods' ilk, he fell off the Tour's radar screen after finishing second at Pebble

David Duval, holder of the course record at Pebble Beach, hits from the 10th fairway on Tuesday.

Tiger Woods discusses his approach shot with caddie Steve Williams during a Tuesday practice round. Woods finished in third place at the 1999 U.S. Open, behind Payne Stewart and Phil Mickelson.

Top: *In his previous outing at the U.S. Open in Pebble Beach in 1992, Scotland's Colin Montgomerie watched his Sunday lead slip away as Tom Kite held on to win.*

Above: *South Africa's Ernie Els, left, a two-time U.S. Open champion and runner-up at the 2000 Masters, waits to tee off on the 18th hole with Nick Price, center, and Greg Norman during a practice round Tuesday.*

Beach in 1982. Resigned to never recovering his once majestic swing, he retired in 1995, and played just one tournament in 21 months prior to the Open.

His road home started with a dinner conversation with Tour pro Bill Glasson during the third week of May. Clampett shared with Glasson his excitement about competing in local Open qualifying the following week in Cary, N.C., where he lives with his wife, Ann, his daughter and two sons.

Clampett shot 73 on a windy day at Prestonwood Country Club, making him the fourth alternate for sectional qualifying, an unlikely position from which to advance any further. The week before the 36-hole sectional qualifying, Clampett, an announcer for CBS, was working the Kemper Open in Potomac, Md., virtually next door to Woodmont Country Club in Rockville. "I slipped over and played a few practice rounds," Clampett said. "I just thought that I better get ready, because you never know. It was so unlikely, but I had faith."

Three days before the June 5 sectional at Woodmont, Clampett got an e-mail from Glasson, who wrote, "I want you to have my spot. I'm not going to qualify."

Clampett was going to show up anyway, and got to the club early to practice. The range was so full he had to walk over among the pine trees and swing at some small pinecones on the ground to warm up. But as he waited, he kept hearing names of alternates being called to the tee, though none arrived. Finally, they called his name.

Tiger Woods, known for his long drives, uses finesse instead of power on the 106-yard seventh hole in a practice round with Mark O'Meara Tuesday.

As it turned out, Clampett did, indeed, get to play in Glasson's place. "I was the fourth alternate," Clampett said, "and he was the fourth one to withdraw. So, I got Billy Glasson's spot. You know, we have been such close friends for so many years," Clampett said. "I think he really wanted me to have a chance to come home to Pebble Beach for the U.S. Open. That's the kind of person he is."

Of course, Glasson couldn't hit any shots for Clampett, who opened with three straight bogeys. But he settled down and played the next 15 holes 7-under-par for a 68, and topped it with a 68 in the afternoon round to made the cut.

Clampett's mother, Jacqueline Clampett-Jones, who bought him his first set of clubs for Christmas when he was 10 and walked thousands of fairways over the years, was happy to have her son home one more time in the U.S. Open. Also, it would be the first time Clampett's children would get to see him play in a major championship. He had already gone through the PGA Tour ranks by the time his daughter, Katelyn, and sons Daniel and Michael were born.

"I told them I wanted them to experience a part of my life they never got to experience," Clampett said.

Javier Sanchez

Javier Sanchez doesn't seem real, but rather a character invented by the USGA to prove that the U.S. Open is truly the world's most democratic sporting event.

In 1976, Sanchez sneaked across the Mexican border using a green card he bought from another man for $50. He was 17, and had grown up on a farm without electricity, running water, or neighbors. To go to school, he commuted more than an hour each way on horseback.

He took a job as a dishwasher in the San Francisco Bay Area, and at 21 picked up a golf club for the first time. At that point, Sanchez was completely unindoctrinated in the ways of golf, having not even seen it played on television.

His introduction to the game came when Sanchez took a job cooking in a restaurant at Palo Alto Municipal Golf Course. "It looked interesting, so I got some used clubs, a bag, and I used to go to the driving range and not even hit a ball but just watched people swing," Sanchez said. "Later on, when everybody would leave, I kind of started imitating.

"I used to putt with the lights on in the parking lot; they'd just shine on the putting green. I used to play there until 9 or 10. And I put in a lot of hard work. Like I said, working hard for me is not a problem."

At the age of 41, Sanchez went through local qualifying to reach the 2000 U.S. Open at the most opulent resort in the world. He still has hopes of reaching the PGA Tour.

"Why not?" Sanchez said. "I left reality behind me a long time ago."

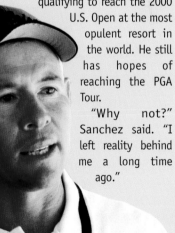

Above: *Mark O'Meara, winner of five AT&T Pebble Beach National Pro-Ams, hits from one of the menacing bunkers on the fourth hole on Tuesday.*

Right: *John Daly's motto-bearing bag lays greenside as Daly putts out on the 12th hole.*

The Past Champions Dinner

The Beach Club at Pebble Beach is accustomed to hosting elite parties, but on Tuesday, June 13, the guest list was so exclusive that not even Tiger Woods could get an invitation.

It was a gathering of past U.S. Open champions, from the oldest living winner, 88-year-old Byron Nelson, to the youngest, 30-year-old Ernie Els. The festivities included a social hour, dinner and an open podium for the players to share their U.S. Open memories.

"This being the 100th U.S. Open, we thought this would be a great opportunity to get all the past champions together at Pebble Beach," said Jerry Pate, the 1976 winner, who worked with the United States Golf Association to coordinate the first reunion of its kind for U.S. Open champions.

While many of the players knew one another, the Past Champions Dinner was a chance for a modern champion like Els, whose second win in 1997 came at Congressional Country Club outside Washington, D.C., to reflect with Ken Venturi, who won there in 1964. Likewise, someone like 1998 winner Lee Janzen could compare notes with the likes of Tommy Bolt, the winner of the 1958 Open.

"These young guys don't want to hear my old stories," said Bolt, as engaging as ever at age 84. "They have their own stories to tell."

Of course, the nine past champions who were at Pebble Beach to compete in the 100th U.S. Open could only shake their heads at Bolt recounting the check he earned for winning the national championship: $8,000. "Can you believe that?" Bolt said. The winner in 2000 would earn $800,000.

As the men congregated, Pate didn't miss the opportunity to educate Els on Bolt. "Terrible Tommy" not only had a Vesuvian temper that would flare up occasionally on the golf course; he had a flair for colorful outfits, as well. "He made Doug Sanders look like a farm boy," Pate said.

Pate served as the unofficial emcee for the evening, and after a few words of welcome from USGA Executive Director David Fay and President Trey Holland, Pate turned the microphone over to any of the players who wanted to share something from his experience as a U.S. Open champion.

Jack Nicklaus and Arnold Palmer were among the guests, as was Tracy Stewart, the widow of two-time champion Payne Stewart, who would have been the defending champion at Pebble Beach.

In all, there were 21 players who attended, each with his wife or guest.

The champions also sat for one of the greatest group photos in the history of golf, in that it portrayed the face of the game for the past eight decades: Nelson, Bolt, Palmer, Nicklaus, Venturi, Tony Jacklin, Johnny Miller, Hale Irwin, Lou Graham, Pate, Andy North, Tom Watson, Larry Nelson, Fuzzy Zoeller, Scott Simpson, Curtis Strange, Tom Kite, Janzen, Els, Corey Pavin, and Steve Jones.

"Having something like this is a wonderful idea," said Jacklin, the 1970 champion and the last European to win the U.S. Open.

"This is such a nice thing to be doing," Bolt said. "I really don't know some of the younger guys, but I always like to see the older guys."

While Simpson and Janzen were two of the younger guys who won at San Francisco's Olympic Club — Simpson holding off Watson in 1987 and Janzen edging Stewart in 1998 — Bolt said he should have won there, too, in 1955, the year Jack Fleck beat Ben Hogan.

"Woooo, was that a tough golf course," Bolt recalled. "I was leading, going into the last two rounds, but I would never make any putts. But that's an old story."

It was one of many stories that the past champions, young and old, enjoyed at the Beach Club.

Past champions Tom Kite, Jack Nicklaus, and Tom Watson with their common legacy — the U.S. Open trophy.

CHAPTER EIGHT

Goodbye, Friend

*Far too soon, the golf community
bid a stirring sunrise farewell
to its lost son.*

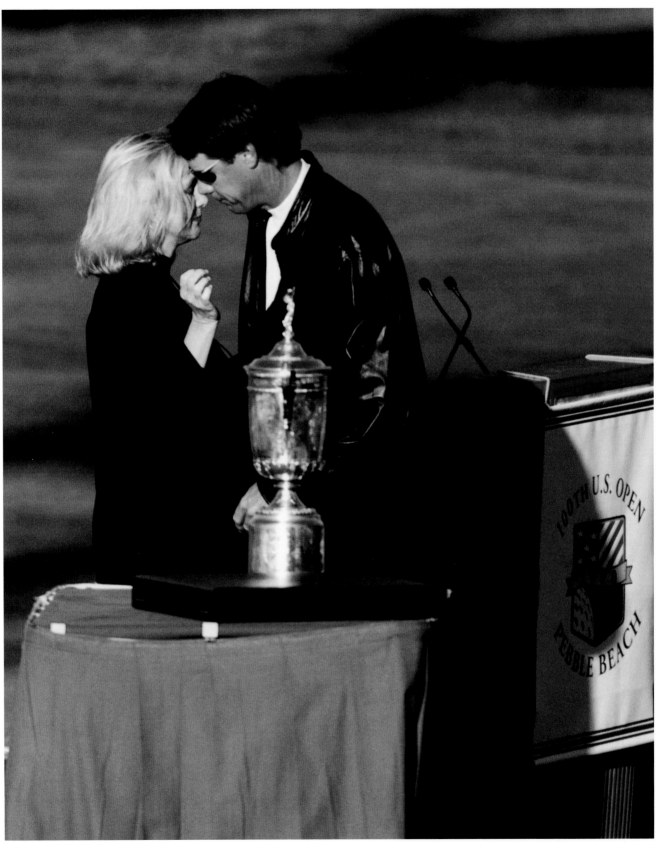

Tracy Stewart and Paul Azinger console one another during the sunrise memorial service for late champion Payne Stewart during Wednesday of Open week. Stewart, the winner of the 1991 and 1999 U.S. Open, as well as the 1999 AT&T Pebble Beach National Pro-Am, died in a plane crash October 25, 1999.

Your finest bottle

On an evening just prior to the start of the 2000 U.S. Open, with the sun bidding farewell for another day and the moon assuming its position to sprinkle a soft glow over Carmel Bay, he walked quietly toward the 18th hole at Pebble Beach Golf Links, the roar of the Pacific Ocean continuous, breathtaking beauty stretched to the dissolving horizon. He carried with him a bottle of expensive champagne, priceless memories, and an indescribable pain to the wall that protects one of golf's most precious pieces of real estate from the fury of nature.

On that wall, golf coach Chuck Cook raised a toast to his friend and pupil Payne Stewart, just as he promised he would in a tearful October eulogy in front of the thousands of people who filled First Baptist Church in Orlando. That morning, less than a week removed from the Lear Jet crash that took the life of the reigning Open champion at the age of 42, along with five others, Cook posed the question: "How do you celebrate the life of the greatest celebrator you know?"

Us and them

In the scope of life, there is us, and there are men like Payne Stewart and Chuck Cook. You know the type: Gatsby-esque golden boys with backlit blue eyes, full of philosophy and wonder and charisma so deep you could jump in and never touch the bottom. So gallant and amusing they made the girls swoon; so athletic and poised they made men do the same. Both zoomed through life checking off items from the Beyond-Your-Wildest-Dreams list. From time to time we'd live with our noses pressed up against the window of their lives.

> *"God is going to call me home sometime, and I'm going to a special place when I die. But I want to make sure my life is special while I'm here."*
>
> — Payne Stewart

Before the 1992 U.S. Open at Pebble Beach, Stewart, the 1991 Open winner, invited Cook to attend a pre-championship media day. Stewart brought the Open trophy along, and left it in his and Cook's room in the Pebble Beach Lodge. Cook remembers the rest of the story like this:

"After playing a round, we went to the Tap Room restaurant. A guy from New Jersey came up to Payne and said, 'Some guy over there said you're Payne Stewart, but I don't believe him.'

"Payne turned to the guy and said, 'If I get the U.S.

A silver bowl full of golf balls awaits a special 21-shot salute to Payne Stewart on the Wednesday prior to the start of play at the U.S. Open.

Open trophy and prove to you I'm Payne Stewart, will you fill it with anything from the bar I want?'

"The guy said, 'Anything and everything.' Payne rushed back to the room, grabbed the trophy and brought it back to the Tap Room. Then he turned to the bartender and said, 'Cristal champagne, please.'

"Me and Payne took the trophy out to the seawall on the 18th hole and sipped it as we laid back and looked up at the stars. We were out there laughing and talking for an hour, and Payne discussed how much he didn't want to have to give the trophy back."

In fact, Tom Kite, another of Cook's pupils, would take the 1992 championship. But just four months prior to his death, Stewart won the 1999 title, slipping past playing partner Phil Mickelson in a Father's Day scramblefest on the famed and treacherous Pinehurst No. 2 course in North Carolina.

"And this time, he doesn't have to give the trophy back," Cook said.

The journey ends

The year 2000 was to have represented Stewart's coronation in the Golf Kingdom. He was expected in

Responding to the call "Ready! Aim! Fire!" U.S. Open participants drive balls into the Pacific Ocean along the 18th fairway at Pebble Beach.

As the sun peeks over Del Monte Forest, golfers watch as their tributary shots land in the Pacific Ocean.

Pebble Beach, first in February and again in June, as the defending champion of both the AT&T Pro-Am and the U.S. Open.

His arrival was to have been the culmination of a spiritual journey.

Two years before his death, one would have presumed by virtue of his appearance that Stewart had his life in order. With his swing antique in rhythm and finish, he was equally classic in dress. He wore a tam-o'-shanter cap and plus-four knickers. He carried a handmade wooden case with 12 pairs of silver-toed, $400 shoes, and had a closet at home dedicated just to his socks. The look was the result of some advice from his outrageous father, Bill, who once told him, "Son, you gotta make 'em remember you."

Stewart's swing and carriage were always perfect. As a person, though, he was far from it. In his early days, he was described by his mother Rose as "rude," by his wife Tracy as "arrogant," and by Stewart himself as "immature."

But Stewart, famous for glaring and preening like a bantam rooster, had recently discovered God and himself. Now he found himself reformed like a modern-day Ebenezer Scrooge on Christmas morning.

Byron Nelson, at 88 the U.S. Open's oldest living champion, watches the salute.

Top: *Tom Lehman and son talk with Tracy Stewart after the ceremony honoring her husband.*

Above: *Tracy Stewart is comforted by an emotional Sergio Garcia.*

Left: *Amy Mickelson, wife of Phil Mickelson, who finished second to Payne Stewart at the 1999 U.S. Open, gives Tracy Stewart a warm embrace.*

75 miles from home

Mike Hicks of Mebane, N.C., was Payne Stewart's caddie for 11 years. Hicks was on the bag when Stewart won the U.S. Open at Hazeltine in 1991, as well as when he faltered after leading in 1993 and 1998. Finally, Hicks was by Stewart's side during his 1999 triumph at Pinehurst No. 2 in North Carolina. Hicks begins his recollections of the final round of the 1999 Open with Stewart leading Phil Mickelson by one stroke heading to the green on No. 18:

Phil was up on the green in regulation, about 25 feet from the cup. Payne, meanwhile, chipped up to within 15 feet. Phil's putt looked real good for a long time, but just missed. He tapped in for par, and at this point I was hoping Payne would just leave it close so we could go to a Monday play-off.

Just leave it close, I thought. Make it to Monday.

Being in my home state, and with all my friends and family watching, little did I know I'd be part of one of the greatest moments in sports. Payne's stroke was perfect, and I could see the label on his ball just rolling over and over and over until it just disappeared.

I paused for a second to see how to react, but Payne was well on his way, doing his fist-pump, Incredible Hulk routine. Man, that guy had a lot of mannerisms! He could get his whole body working somehow.

It was classic Payne.

All I could think to do was run. Spontaneously, I leapt into his arms. He was yelling in my ear, "You beauty! Oh, you beauty!"

We didn't get done with the media until 10 p.m. Unbelievably, Payne had made a commitment to play a round at my home club, Mill Creek, in Mebane, N.C., which is 75 miles from Pinehurst. I couldn't believe it, but he still wanted to come.

My buddy, a North Carolina highway patrolman, gave us a police escort all the way home. While another friend drove, Payne and I sat in the back seat and sipped some beers. I wanted the trip to last, so we took some back roads home. Every so often, we'd pull over in some Andy Griffith town to get some more beer or do our business. At one point, we got out at Siler City, the smallest of small towns. There were 30 miles of country roads before we hit civilization. Payne got out of the car, and he was incognito without his knickers or funny hat.

We went into a convenience store to pick up a 12-pack

of beer, and as we stood at the counter, my police buddy asked the clerk, "Aren't you going to ask for his ID?"

"No, he looks old enough to drink," she said, pointing at Payne.

"You sure you don't want to know who this man is?" my buddy asked.

"No, it's OK," she replied.

"Well, I'll tell you," he said. "This man, Payne Stewart, just committed the biggest robbery that ever happened in this state."

About 20 people stayed at my house that night, and we stayed up until about 4:30 a.m. Every time I tried to go to bed, Payne just told me, "You'll sleep when I say you can sleep."

The next morning, I woke up not feeling too good, and walked into my front hall. Down the stairs came Payne, fresh as the new day, in his little get-up. There he was, Payne Stewart, the U.S. Open champion in all his splendor, just grinning.

He was my friend.

"I see coming to Pebble Beach as a symbol of my rebirth," Stewart said in a September 1999 interview. "To wear the champion's crown there will mean more to me than just simply as a golfer."

Sadly, the guards at the kingdom's gate wore black cotton gloves the day Stewart died. The clocks stopped, the drums were muffled and the horns silenced. The stars were dimmed, the moon packed in, the ocean put away and the woods swept up. The morning clouds above, which surely would have parted for his arrival, scribbled against the sky, "He's gone."

The last goodbye

On Wednesday, June 14, a day before Open play began, the clouds did part to provide a morning that not even the best words could describe. At a sunrise service along the most spectacular finishing hole in golf — the same one on which Stewart and Cook celebrated that night eight years before — golf's royalty bid Stewart a final official farewell. In a ceremony reminiscent of a 21-gun salute, golfers responding to the call "Ready!...Aim!...Fire!" choked back tears and splashed balls into the Pacific in a poignant tribute to their fallen friend.

Tracy Stewart, ever graceful, delivered a stirring eulogy to the hundreds of fans and friends in attendance. "The past couple of months have been extremely hard," she said. "There is a void in my heart that only Payne can fill. But my message to you today is about hope. Payne never lost hope. He inspired us all."

Paul Azinger, Stewart's best friend, shared a prophetic quote from Stewart, himself, in reference to his two children.

"Payne said, 'If, on the way home something happens to me, and I can't play golf, I've had a wonderful career,'" Azinger quoted. "'I want to spend the rest of my life with my family. I want to give them all the love I can. God is going to call me home sometime, and I'm going to a special place when I die. But I want to make sure my life is special while I'm here.'"

There is a common thread between men like Chuck Cook and ourselves: God forbid we lose our friends. Ceremonies like Stewart's farewell reinforce the fundamental truth that, as the poet wrote, life may keep us apart. It may prevent us from thinking of each other very often. But we know our friend is out there — where, we don't know — far away, but deeply faithful. We wait for our paths to cross again, to greet each other joyfully and to shake each other by the shoulders.

For now, though, we must get used to waiting.

Phil Mickelson

On Father's Day 1999, Phil Mickelson strode over the fairways of Pinehurst No. 2 with a shot at the U.S. Open championship and a beeper on his belt. Had the beeper sounded, Mickelson said, he would have walked off the course immediately with the intent of being at the bedside of his wife, Amy, for the birth of their first child.

Amanda Brynn Mickelson waited, and arrived the next day. She allowed her famous father to battle Payne Stewart all the way to the 72nd hole.

Stewart, a father of two himself, won the tournament with a dramatic 15-foot putt on No. 18. The notion of a storybook ending, with Mickelson bringing the Open trophy home to his newborn, was dashed.

Stewart bear-hugged his caddie, then whirled and grabbed both sides of Mickelson's face. "Good luck with the baby!" he shouted. "There's nothing like being a father!"

"Right then, it changed my feeling about the disappointment I'd just felt to what I was looking forward to," Mickelson said a year later prior to the start of the 2000 Open. "The birth of this child, influencing this person in this world. And Payne made it apparent at that moment that fatherhood was what was more important to him, too."

A year later, with three days to go until his daughter's first birthday and his first Father's Day, Mickelson had a heightened awareness of how Stewart felt at Pinehurst.

"It's been more difficult for my wife and me to keep our family together, with all my travel," Mickelson said. "But fatherhood is so fulfilling. Today, I can tell you that winning the Open is the second-most important thing to me."

Serenity returned to the 18th fairway at Pebble Beach following the tribute to Payne Stewart. Stewart celebrated his 1991 U.S. Open win by drinking champagne with coach Chuck Cook along the hole's seawall.

Top: *David Frost and Chris Walkey flank a standard-bearer for a photo on the seventh hole on Wednesday.*

Left: *Jack Nicklaus reacts to reaching the green on the fifth hole, which he designed. At the behest of partner Andy Bean, it took Nicklaus five tries to hit the green.*

Above: *Mark O'Meara and Tiger Woods watch the foursome ahead while they wait for their turn to tee off on No. 10.*

The caddie is a champ

Andy Martinez caddied for Johnny Miller during his glory days, and was on the bag for 17 of Miller's 24 PGA Tour wins, including the 1973 U.S. Open and the Pebble Beach National Pro-Am in 1974 and 1994.

It was at Pebble Beach, in fact, that Martinez met Monterey Peninsula native Bobby Clampett in 1982. Miller generously split Martinez with Clampett that season — 15 tournaments each — and Clampett went on to record his only career Tour win at the Southern Open.

Martinez then picked up with Tom Lehman, who promptly won the British Open in 1996. The duo came to Pebble Beach in November 1998, and won the Callaway Pebble Beach Invitational, a prestigious off-season event. In fact, it was Martinez's second Callaway win, as he also helped Bob Gilder to victory in 1988.

Finally, Martinez was by the side of 20-year-old David Gossett, a University of Texas sophomore, when he won the 99th U.S. Amateur at Pebble Beach in 1999, handily defeating Sung Yoon Kim 9 and 8 in the finals.

Martinez may not be in a class by himself when it comes to looping Pebble Beach. But whatever class he's in, it doesn't take long to call roll.

"I can't explain my success at Pebble Beach," Martinez said. "It is sort of odd. I guess the course and I sort of speak to each other."

Whatever is being said, Martinez is getting the message loud and clear. Under tournament conditions, Pebble Beach plays like a cruel mistress, and invokes in players their tempestuous worst.

Yet according to his bosses, Martinez, 50, is able to see free and clear of such distractions. On greens with more cuts than a line of first-graders for recess, Martinez knows the breaks. Where there are fairways that dogleg so severely you'd swear they were designed in a kennel, Martinez knows the shortcuts. And where there is grass so tall that players discover why they call it "rough," Martinez knows when to run it and when to gun it.

"Andy is by far the most meticulous caddie on the Tour," said Lehman, whose bag Martinez would carry at the 2000 Open. "Sometimes he'll tell you to hit, say, a 5-iron. I'll start to argue with a 'C'mon, Andy, let's hit a —,' and then I'll remember who I'm talking to and just say, 'Sorry, man. A 5 it is.' "

It was Martinez's attention to detail that brought him to Gossett. The two met in June 1999, at the St. Jude Classic in Memphis.

"In a casual conversation, I asked David if he'd ever been out to Pebble Beach and if he had a caddie for the week," Martinez said. "Then I found out I had the week off."

Martinez confessed he had an ulterior motive.

"I wanted to see Pebble Beach under USGA conditions on Tom's behalf," Martinez said.

Despite the fact that carrying Gossett's bag was only a part-time job, Martinez committed to it fully.

"At the start of the Amateur, David and Andy were very professional," said Pam Gossett, David's mother. "But by Sunday, they were staying up late, playing cards and watching 'America's Funniest Home Videos.' Andy was calling David his 'little man.' You just get the sense that he's the best there is when it comes to understanding Pebble and the relaxed mindset it takes to win there."

From Gossett's victory, Martinez took his customary 10 percent of total earnings — which, because it was the Amateur, amounted to the princely sum of $0. Despite having been over the course hundreds of times, Martinez at least hoped he'd gained a greater sense of Pebble Beach than he had before.

"You always want your guy to be able to play the course, rather than the opponent," Martinez said. "To know Pebble is to have a relationship with it, to feel it. You can't let go and then come back. It always has to be tended to."

An unfamiliar sight on the normally regal Seventeen Mile Drive, Chris and Brian Orosco tout practice round parking for spectators at their family's home located just above the first green.

Left: *A ticketholder tries to sell his U.S. Open passes along Highway 1 near the seaside town of Moss Landing, approximately 30 miles north of Pebble Beach.*

Above: *Ken Fogarty and his 18-month-old daughter, Kayden, traveled from Orange County to see the final day of U.S. Open practice rounds.*

Above: *Groundskeeper Scott Hollister rakes up the rough around the eighth hole, careful to avoid the cliffs and crashing waves below.*

Left: *Harbor seals sun themselves on rocks in Stillwater Cove on Wednesday, far below the sixth green at Pebble Beach.*

CHAPTER NINE

A New Low

A flawless opening round of golf by Tiger Woods at the 2000 U.S. Open was a harbinger of things to come, yet had been years in the making.

Tiger Woods and Jesper Parnevik mark their balls in tandem on the second green during the first round of the 2000 U.S. Open. Woods did not three-putt the entire round en route to a record first-round low 65.

Bear tracks

It is said that all great thoroughbreds are descended from three Arabian stallions. The same could be said for the modern golfer and Jack Nicklaus. From the start, the Golden Bear's style and unbelievable string of victories inspired thousands of young cubs, and one Tiger.

When Eldrick (Tiger) Woods was 11, he spent an entire afternoon constructing a chart to mount over his bed in Cypress, Calif. Down the left-hand column he carefully wrote the names of all the major golf tournaments. Then he cut a photo of Nicklaus out from a magazine and placed it at the top of another column; below it he penciled in Nicklaus' age at the time he won each major for the first time: U.S. Open — 22, Masters — 23, PGA Championship — 23, British Open — 26. Finally, Woods wrote his own name at the top of the third column.

He was not simply an athlete. He was Bobby Fisher at the chess board, Wolfgang Amadeus Mozart at the piano.

"I want to become the youngest player ever to win all the majors," Woods told his father, Earl. "I want to do all the things Jack did before he did them."

After he won his first U.S. Amateur championship in August 1994, Woods returned home to Cypress and found a pencil. He approached his chart and slid his finger down to the line that read U.S. AMATEUR, then across to the column beneath his name. There he wrote his age: 18 YEARS, 8 MONTHS. He had won the Amateur one month before Nicklaus had.

The rest of the chart awaited.

An unquiet life

Earl and Tida Woods tended Tiger as if he were the last rose in their garden. Even as a child he breathed the air of prophesy, and it had become fact to him, part of his marrow. He was not simply an athlete. He was Bobby Fisher at the chess board, Wolfgang Amadeus Mozart at the piano.

Right away there were signs. At six months he could balance in his father's palm. At 11 months he could pick up a sawed-off club, imitate Earl's golf swing and drive the ball into a nylon net across the garage. At age 4, Earl would drop him off at the golf course at 9 a.m. on a Saturday and pick him up at 5 p.m. to find his pockets full of change he had won from disbelieving elders.

Los Angeles freelance television reporter Jim Gray

Spain's Sergio Garcia wears knickers on opening day in honor of Payne Stewart. A frustrated Garcia said other European players promised to also wear knickers on Thursday, but failed to follow through.

People strolling along Carmel Beach watch first-round play on the ninth green and 10th fairway at Pebble Beach. The eighth, ninth, and 10th holes at Pebble Beach are referred to as the "Cliffs of Doom," as their intricacies and exposure to the elements can turn a round from good to bad.

Above: *Hal Sutton, who took an early lead after scoring an eagle on the first hole Thursday, launches his approach shot over the deep chasm on No. 8.*

Right: *John Huston tees off on the 17th hole. Huston came out strong at the Open, ending the day with a first-round 67.*

Bobby Clampett

He never knew how precious the gift was until he lost it.

And then he got it back, if only for just one day.

"It was," 40-year-old Bobby Clampett said, "like playing golf in heaven." Indeed, whereas Moses came down from the mountain, Clampett came down from the tower.

For Clampett, known primarily as an announcer for CBS since 1995, it was a return to the wellspring. Playing Pebble Beach, a course onto which he snuck a hundred times as a teenager growing up in nearby Carmel Valley, Clampett had a share of the lead at the U.S. Open partway into the first round. This wouldn't have raised eyebrows 20 years ago, when he was one of the best young golfers in the world. But now that seemed like another lifetime ago.

It was at Pebble Beach in 1972 that Clampett shagged balls for Jack Nicklaus and hitched a ride home with Arnold Palmer. He went on to win two State Amateur titles there, and tied for third, behind Tom Watson and Nicklaus, at the 1982 Open.

Then it all went wrong. Mr. Can't Miss missed. Clampett got too deep into his swing mechanics and lost his natural gift.

"Bobby could have done what Tiger Woods has done," said Ben Doyle, Clampett's first teacher who now works at Quail Lodge in Carmel Valley. "He used to be able to hit a ball on one leg and look artistic. But he became so mechanical, so robotlike, with so many screwy ways of hitting the ball."

Clampett fell to 64th on the money list in 1983, and then to 117th in 1984. He continued to spiral downward, reaching his last Open in 1986, and effectively retired in 1995. His last competitive tournament of any kind was the 1998 Buick Challenge, where he missed the cut.

In January 2000, Clampett had dinner one evening with fellow broadcaster Ken Venturi. Venturi, a former Open champion himself, had been asked to captain the Presidents Cup competition, and Clampett asked kiddingly what he must do to make the team.

"He said, 'Win the Open,' " Clampett recalled. "And I said, 'OK. That's my dream. I'm going to play in one tournament this year and let's see if we can get into it.' "

After pounding balls on his spacious lawn at home in Cary, N.C., Clampett miraculously reached the 2000 Open by way of local qualifying. And in that fateful first Open round, his gift returned as mysteriously as it had disappeared.

"I never met anybody's expectations," Clampett said, "nor my own. Then to suddenly be hitting great shots — well, they were some of the best golf shots I'd ever hit."

Clampett didn't miss a green or fairway over the first 10 holes, and finished with a 3-under par 68.

"When I made my putt on 9 for birdie — a putt that would have gone 10 feet past the cup if it hadn't gone in — I looked up and thanked God. My eyes welled with tears. It was amazing."

In just one round, Clampett proved the only thing in sport more thrilling than the fulfillment of prophesy is the fulfillment of the unexpected.

Jesper Parnevik hits his second shot on the ninth hole from a side-hill lie as fans in the grandstand look on.

Mark O'Meara and his caddie wait on the ninth fairway for the chance to approach the green, as fishermen go about their duties behind them.

took notice when he saw in the agate section of the *L.A. Times* that an Eldrick Woods of Cypress, age 4, had made his fourth hole-in-one. Gray filmed a segment in which Woods looked straight into the camera and said, "I will be the greatest golfer ever." Gray concluded his piece by saying that Woods would be to golf what "Jimmy Connors and Chris Evert have been to tennis."

Gray's report turned Woods into a celebrity. A few months later he appeared on *The Mike Douglas Show*, upstaging Bob Hope in a driving contest. At 5, he was featured on *That's Incredible*.

Success became an echo for Woods, a tuning fork he could strike himself. At the age of 11, Woods went undefeated in Southern California junior events, some 30 tournaments in all, most with fields of over 100 players. By his teens he had played at St. Andrews with Sam Snead, been presented a trophy by Lee Trevino, and teed it up in exhibitions with Nicklaus, Greg Norman and John Daly. At 16 years and two months, he became the youngest ever to play in a PGA Tour event (the 1992 L.A. Open, where he briefly debuted the Tiger Paw — a catlike clawing gesture he used to punctuate the dropping of a putt); the youngest ever

Phil Mickelson lines up a putt on No. 14's postage-stamp green that slopes sharply back toward the fairway.

and the first African-American to win the U.S. Amateur (at age 18, four years younger than Bobby Jones when he won his first Amateur); the first male to win three U.S. Juniors; and the first male to win the Junior and the Amateur.

Woods began looking at golf courses the way a bow looks at strings. Indeed, he was becoming so well-known that it was as if he was learning to play violin on a street corner — everyone was aware of his progress.

The prophesy

So far that winter day in 1995, Tiger Woods had won the Masters, played his first British Open, led the U.S. Open wire-to-wire and finished an Economics paper.

> *Woods began looking at golf courses the way a bow looks at strings. Indeed, he was becoming so well-known that it was as if he was learning to play violin on a street corner — everyone was aware of his progress.*

"Here's Woods, 13th tee box, Augusta National, Sunday," the Stanford freshman said, waggling his club at the university's driving range. "A 19-year-old who just happens to be the first black to win the Masters. Would that be a story?" Woods then hooded his ball into the trees along the makeshift fairway. "Now here's Woods asking his caddie for another ball.

"All right, Pebble Beach, U.S. Open, Tiger Woods one shot ahead of Mr. Strange, two holes to play. Mr. Strange making an amazing comeback today. Woods needs two perfect drives here..."

"Tiger," a sportswriter interrupted, "are you the next Jack Nicklaus?"

"Nope," he said, "The first Tiger Woods."

Even then, Woods showed signs of needing to establish his own identity. The ghost of Jack Nicklaus had become a tough Bear to cross.

The legend grows

What Woods had done since turning pro in 1996 is the stuff of legend. Leading up to the 2000 Open, he had 19 career wins — including a 5-stroke victory two weeks before at Nicklaus' Memorial Tournament — and was the leading money winner in Tour history at age 24. Woods was coming off a 1999 season in which he'd won eight tournaments, and four straight to end the year. He'd extended that streak into the next millennium, running off two more wins to start 2000.

Jon "Tin Cup" Levitt

When a 37-year-old driving-range pro qualified for his first-ever U.S. Open, the media immediately nicknamed him "Tin Cup," after the character Kevin Costner played in a movie by the same name.

With a shaved head and a dangling earring, Jon Levitt, of Long Beach, Calif., didn't look a whole lot like Costner — nor did he play like the fictional Roy "Tin Cup" McAvoy — but his personality was pure Hollywood.

The outgoing, self-effacing Levitt cavorted easily with the spectators, some of whom recognized him from the media coverage.

"We were walking down one of the fairways and these two old guys were sitting there with tee-time sheets," Levitt said after Friday's round. "And one of them yells, 'Hey, I know who this one is — that's Tin Can! I mean, Tin Cup!'"

Levitt, once a Nike Tour pro, had played Pebble Beach before — but never when the course was in U.S. Open condition, with daunting rough and murderous greens — and never with the stakes so high.

"This was like walking on holy ground for me today," he said after his round Thursday. "Pebble Beach is such a special place, and I'm just happy to be out here right now."

With his friend and caddie, Joe O'Neill, snapping pictures, Levitt thoroughly enjoyed his first two days, but frustration set in on Wednesday, when he played an awful practice round.

And his angst increased when championship play began.

Levitt was 4 over par with two holes to play in Thursday's opening round, but bogeyed 17 and triple-bogeyed 18, virtually erasing any chance he may have had of making the cut the following day.

On Friday, in the second round, he played a bit better, but bowed out at 15-over for the tournament.

"That's why I'm Tin Cup this week," he said with a shrug, "and not some other guy the media should be talking to."

Top: *Paul Azinger flexes his muscle as fitness fanatic David Duval walks past on the second tee.*

Above: *Caddie Pete Bender reacts to Rocco Mediate's club selection.*

By June, he'd won 11 of his last 20 starts and 15 of his last 26. Winning had become as inevitable as gravity; his streaks could no longer be considered streaks. Undaunted by his explosive celebrity, Woods seemed less interested in having his ring kissed than in repeatedly dominating everyone within the kingdom. The rest of the Tour had seen the future and it was second place.

Moreover, Woods had done for golf what spring does for the cherry trees. By way of his charisma and visceral fist-pumping, golf was experiencing a Renaissance. To understand what golf had become, it was not necessary to watch Tiger Woods. Rather, one needed to watch who was watching Tiger Woods. Everyone from barrister to bartender, CEO to mother with a stroller was making his or her way to the course to see the young man who was arguably the best golfer of all time.

"Arguably." That's what got to Woods. His six consecutive wins were impressive, but it was a jag matched by Ben Hogan in 1948. Furthermore, Woods' number was just more than half of Byron Nelson's DiMaggio-like 11 set in 1945. His eight-win season was a thing of beauty, but couldn't touch golf's Holy Trinity — Nelson's 18 victories in 1945, Bobby Jones'

Grand Slam in 1930, and Hogan's Masters, U.S. Open, and British Open victories in 1953. Certainly, Woods had won the 1997 Masters by a monstrous 12 strokes and the 1999 PGA Championship by an eyelash, but Nicklaus' record 18 majors seemed comparatively daunting.

Woods, on the other hand — the man with the thunderous drives and the velveteen touch; the man of mixed heritage who made Black-Thai no longer optional in golfing circles — was born to symbolize a revolution.

Golf inflicts pain on those who play it, and there are no exceptions. The game answers back. Besides his four victories in 2000, he had chances to win the Buick Invitational, the Nissan Open, and the World Match Play, but didn't. Hal Sutton outplayed him at the Players Championship, he stumbled at the Masters, and blew a two-shot lead to Lee Westwood in Germany. That's just how golf is, even for the contenders.

But Woods wanted to change all that, and saw the 2000 Open as his forum. He wanted to win the national championship on command, and by gobs, not gasps. Rumor had it he was sleeping with the Open record book by his bedside, and had his eye on exceeding Willie Smith's mammoth 11-stroke victory in 1899, and also wanted to crack 272 — the Open's holy grail established by Nicklaus in 1980.

New frontier

Woods had come to realize that a well-honed game would stand the test of time better than his ephemeral lightning bolts. Thus, from hard work he wrought a more repeatable swing. A demarcation of the new frontier came at Pebble Beach in February, when Woods came back from seven strokes down with seven holes to play to score the most astonishing comeback in recent memory. See, Woods seemed to say, I can make the game bend to me.

Woods stood on the precipice of two great accomplishments. First, by winning the 2000 U.S. and British Opens, he could become the youngest of five players — Ben Hogan, Gene Sarazen, Jack Nicklaus and Gary Player being the others — to win the career Grand Slam. Second, he could for once get ahead of his own legend. He could once again produce the unexpected.

Jesper Parnevik

In a perfect world, they would all be like Jesper Parnevik. Every guy on Tour would dress like a paint store blew up all over him, and grin like a Dentyne runway model, especially around his fans.

Indeed, whereas the hordes arrived Thursday to watch Tiger Woods, they left remembering his playing partner wearing the Halloween-orange shirt, which Woods referred to as "our beacon in the fog."

Parnevik, the man who consumes regular doses of volcanic ash to exfoliate his innards, who made the rounds at the 2000 Buick Classic in salmon-pink hot pants, and who characteristically flips up the bill of his ballcap to get a better tan, is the Volkswagen full of clowns in the funeral procession of desensitized celebrity athletes.

What else should we expect from the son of Sweden's best-known comedian?

Is Parnevik a showboat? More than likely, he is simply the rarest and most genuine kind of flake.

He named his oldest daughter Peg, which is what they call a golf tee in his native country. His middle child is named Penny, because that's what Daddy uses to mark his golf balls on the putting green.

And his youngest? Her name is Pebble Peach.

"Oh, that," Jesper explains. "Well, someone suggested we name her Pebbles, someone else wanted to name her Peach. So she's Pebble Peach. Seemed like a good idea at the time."

Tiger Woods hits his approach shot on the ninth hole with Carmel Beach as the backdrop.

Tiger Woods waits on the tee to play Pebble Beach's new No. 5 hole.

Jack Nicklaus tapped his son, Jack II, to be his caddie for his 44th and final U.S. Open.

He would no longer be the "next" anything. He would end golf as we knew it. Nicklaus, after all, was Jones' heir. Charlie Nicklaus raised Jack to emulate Jones, and Jones lived on through Jack. On the other hand, Woods — the man with the thunderous drives and the velveteen touch; the man of mixed heritage who brought the white curtain down on golf — was born to symbolize a revolution.

Heightened focus

Woods arrived at Pebble Beach under the trance of spoon-bending concentration. On the eve of the Open, he spent extra time on the practice green even though he was putting well. "I didn't like the way I was rolling the ball," he said. "I was making quite a few putts in practice rounds, but the ball wasn't turning over the way I like to see it roll."

No less an authority than NHL coach Scotty Bowman, a winner of eight Stanley Cups who was in Woods' practice-round gallery, was wowed at Woods' single-mindedness. "His eye contact is right with his caddie and nowhere else. He's not even conscious of the other players."

A new low

While Woods may not have been aware of them, the other players in the 2000 Open field were conscious of him. When Woods' first-round score was posted Thursday, a buzz ripped through Pebble Beach, from the galleries to the press tent to the posh patio parties. By listening closely, one could detect the words: "It's over."

Tiger Woods reacts as his approach shot on the eighth hole rolls off the back of the green. It was the first green he missed in regulation during the first round of the Open.

David Duval waits out a fog delay from the middle of the 14th fairway at Pebble Beach. Thursday's play was suspended with half the field still on the course.

Above: *Spectators leave after Thursday's play was suspended due to fog.*

Far right: *Kirk Triplett attempts to see around a fog bank while on the 16th fairway.*

Near right: *Signs gave spectators relief from the confusion created by suspended play.*

His morning 65, giving him a one-shot lead over Miguel Angel Jimenez, left the other participants in awe.

"I see Tiger is 6-under," Phil Mickelson said. "I thought anybody under par would be playing great today."

It was the best Open round of Woods' career and the lowest round at the Open since 1980, when Nicklaus and Tom Weiskopf each shot first-round 63s at Baltusrol.

"I saw Steve (Williams, Woods' caddie) pacing off yardage markers, bunkers, ice cream stands that just shouldn't come into play," said Jesper Parnevik, Woods' playing partner. "His is a different world."

It seemed Woods, the master of the dramatic comeback, was trying to avoid such theatrics at the 100th Open.

It was a tamer Tiger's typical round: six birdies, a dozen pars, including six holes where he missed the green and scrambled to save strokes. He never three-putted. His bogey-free round included four birdies on the back nine.

"I played well all day," Woods said. "I can't explain it, but I felt this amazing sense of calm. If you asked me to go through my round, I might not be able to, I was so focused on each shot. But I like that I have one shot to play with."

As if on cue after Woods' round ended, afternoon fog billowed in and surrounded the Monterey Peninsula in a cold shroud that enveloped the seaside holes like a blanket pulled up to the chin. Suddenly, the weather was more appropriate for the commission of a crime than for golf. More likely would there be an appearance by Jack the Ripper than Jack Nicklaus.

Play was halted at 3:57 p.m. Thursday, but wasn't called for the day for more than two hours. Of those who finished, John Huston shot an opening-round 67 to stand two-back, while Monterey Peninsula native Bobby Clampett posted a 68.

A number of prominent players struggled on the first day of play. Sergio Garcia, wearing knickers to honor late champion Payne Stewart, opened with a 75, as did David Duval. Mark O'Meara, winner of five Pebble Beach Pro-Ams, shot 74, and Nick Price shot 77.

Woods stood three rounds from eliminating the margin between him and history. No one had ever gotten off to a better start at Pebble Beach and, goodness, did Woods know how to finish.

John Daly

When John Daly first arrived on Tour, winning the PGA Championship in 1991, a number of media outlets compared him to Jack Nicklaus. Golf magazines ran their pictures side-by-side, illustrating their similarly huge hip turns and audacious backswings. Nicklaus generously agreed that Daly might be the chosen one to assume the Golden Bear's mantle as the architect of the modern game.

At Pebble Beach, both bid farewell to the U.S. Open. However, their exits — like their lives — could not have been more different. Eventually, Nicklaus, ever the sportsman, would be carried out on the lilt of the gallery's applause. A day earlier, Daly saw his five-year exemption by way of his 1995 British Open win come to an end.

That fateful day, Daly arrived at the No. 18 tee box 3-over par with every chance of making the cut. His first tee shot into the fog was three feet out-of-bounds. His subsequent two drives went into the Pacific. Reeling, Daly scored a 14 on the hole and an 83 for the day. On his way from the scorer's tent, he told USGA official Jeff Hall, "Withdraw me from tomorrow's round."

It was the third time Daly, who has battled addiction throughout his career, behaved in such a manner at an Open. He walked off the course during the second round in 1997, and in 1999 took an 11 on the eighth hole at Pinehurst No. 2, at one point taking a penalty for hitting his ball on the green while it was still moving.

As was the case in previous years, Daly drew the ire of the nearly 8,500 entrants who failed to qualify for the event at Pebble Beach. Said first alternate Ty Armstrong: "I feel this way: withdraw once, and it's easier to withdraw twice. I've never done it. I've always finished my obligations."

CHAPTER TEN

The Last Bear Hug

*Pebble Beach cradled Jack Nicklaus
one last time Friday as he ended
an astonishing Open career.*

As he waits for the first round to be continued Friday, Greg Norman considers his lie in an eighth-hole bunker. Norman would miss his third Open cut in a row.

First refusal

Gentleman golfer Bobby Jones once refused to attend a U.S. Amateur Championship.

His son, Robert T. Jones III, was facing Jack Nicklaus, then a junior at Ohio State, in the opening round of match play at Pebble Beach in 1961. At the start of the match, the younger Jones walked across the first tee box and greeted Nicklaus with a warm smile.

"You might be interested to know, Jack," he said, "that my father was thinking of coming out for this tournament. Then when he found out who I had drawn as my first opponent, he changed his mind. He decided it wasn't worth a trip just to see me play one round."

Nicklaus would go on to defeat Jones, and eventually take his second Amateur championship. When he stormed the field that year at Pebble Beach, it appeared as if Nicklaus were God's template for a golfer — audacious in some places, soft as honey in others. Nicklaus did not simply play golf that week. He *was* golf.

Much had changed at Pebble Beach in the 39 years between his Amateur win and the 2000 Open. But much had remained the same.

The course remained as taunting, with its greens unfurling like mocking tongues, daring golfers to enter. And Nicklaus, whose spectacular career would include 44 U.S. Open starts and four victories, remained Pebble Beach's Sphinx, his youthful aura frozen and suspended above its sprawling ramparts.

Friday, June 16, would represent another round of good-byes. There would be the farewell to Nicklaus, playing his record 44th and final Open on the same course where he won the Amateur, the 1972 national championship, and three Crosby Pro-Ams. Also, golf as it had been known was getting a grand send-off, courtesy of Tiger Woods, who contributed a second consecutive day of virtuoso play on the world's premier stage as he continued to reinvent the game.

Out of a fog

Pebble Beach remained shrouded in a clammy gauze as day broke Friday. Seventy-five players had to arrive at the course at 6:45 a.m. to resume their Thursday rounds, then wait another 90 minutes for the fog to lift.

Tears would eventually flow as Nicklaus, in the midst of his worst Open round ever, would make his ceremonial final walk up Pebble Beach's 18th fairway. But before that could happen, the course had other players breaking down for another reason.

The sea breeze that finally shooed away the fog also brought out the beast in Pebble Beach, especially the greens that turned into crusty parcels of concrete with a hazy yellow sheen. The course showed a nasty

Kirk Triplett stretches on the 16th hole, waiting for the resumption of play Friday.

temper, with fickle winds drying the landscape and making par a pleasure.

"You could hear the greens yelling, 'I'm thirsty!'" said Lee Janzen, who had a 73 for a 2-over 144 total.

Greg Norman went eight straight holes with a bogey or worse for an 82, his worst Open ever. He missed the cut for the third straight time. Davis Love would go down for the third time in his career, as would Jesper Parnevik.

Global search

All corners of the globe were trying to catch Woods, who held a one-shot advantage but had to wait nearly 30 hours between his final putt Thursday and his first tee shot Friday afternoon.

Miguel Angel Jimenez, the Spaniard whom Woods beat in a play-off at Valderrama in November, made par on the first five holes and picked up his lone birdie on the par-5 sixth hole. Angel Cabrera of Argentina

Marshals confer during the fog delay on the morning of the second round.

Tom Oliver from Wilmington, Delaware, relaxes near the putting green at The Lodge, as players and fans negotiate another fog delay Friday morning.

U.S. Open spectators wait to cross the fourth fairway after the fog finally parted Friday. While play was to have started at 6:45, it did not begin again until 9 a.m.

Top: *Scores continued to come crashing down Friday, as Kirk Triplett reacts to his chip on 18 sticking to the rough around the greens.*

Right: *Loren Roberts was among a number of golfers who felt the greens were too dry. Here he reacts to a missed putt on the 13th hole.*

Far right: *Colin Montgomerie grimaces as his par putt on 13 falls short.*

Far left: *Hale Irwin, playing on his last U.S. Open exemption, reflects the sentiment of the rest of the field as his chip on the 16th hole races past the cup.*

Left: *A frustrated Vijay Singh takes a stroll through knee-high thicket along the sixth fairway.*

Below: *Nick Faldo provided a rare moment of levity Friday, playing with geese along the 18th fairway.*

Caddie Steve Williams and Tiger Woods examine a putt on No. 2. Woods, after waiting 30 hours between rounds, built a three-stroke advantage over Miguel Angel Jimenez before his round was called on the 12th hole due to darkness.

and Thomas Bjorn of Denmark were both at 2-under. Besides that trio, however, no one else could make a move on Woods. By late afternoon, only three players managed to break par.

Tiger rolls on

The players' struggles in the morning and afternoon provided a stirring contrast for Woods' evening performance. True, it was Nicklaus' day, but Woods would have the final word.

The 24-year-old, playing in his 100th professional tournament at the 100th U.S. Open, had a chance to succumb to the torturous conditions — or take a huge step toward becoming the first wire-to-wire champion since Payne Stewart at Hazeltine in 1991.

Woods was standing on the practice green when he heard the fans roaring as Nicklaus came up the 18th. "It would have been nice seeing it, but I had more important things to take care of," Woods said.

After his first bogey of the championship, on the par-3 fifth hole that Nicklaus built two years before, Woods ripped an iron from the rough on No. 6, the ball climbing over the ocean and a cypress tree and landing on the green 15 feet away for a two-putt birdie.

He birdied the 106-yard seventh hole with a 10-

Football analyst John Madden, a resident of Carmel, was among a number of celebrities to tail Tiger Woods on Friday.

Hands on hips, an exhausted David Duval awaits his final shot of the first round. The No. 2 player in the world would finish with a 75, 10 shots back of Tiger Woods. Duval would recover with an afternoon 71, but would still be 12 shots behind Woods.

Jack Nicklaus savors the moment on No. 18 before teeing off for the last time in a U.S. Open championship.

Fans standing 10-deep greet Nicklaus as he comes up the 18th fairway.

footer, and did the same on the 11th. As the siren sounded signifying play was to be suspended due to darkness, Woods was given the option of finishing out on the 12th hole, and he did so in style. He rapped in a 30-foot putt, his fifth birdie of the round under impossible conditions, and built a three-stroke advantage over Jimenez.

The Walk

They were perched on balconies and hanging out of windows. They ribboned 10 deep along the fairway, and thousands more packed the grandstands behind the 18th green. Each took it upon himself to fill Jack Nicklaus' ears with sustained applause, to make the lower lip of the best Open player ever quiver spontaneously.

On the greatest finishing hole in all of golf, Jack Nicklaus was saying his last good-bye.

"Will I smell the flowers?" Nicklaus said in a Tuesday interview. "No, I'd probably sneeze too much. But will I enjoy this week? Yes, because it's Pebble Beach. And if I was going to pick a spot to play my last U.S. Open, I would pick Pebble Beach.

"This is the place I started in many ways," Nicklaus said, alluding to his 1961 Amateur victory. "About 40 years later, it's a pretty fitting place to stop."

Nicklaus had a premonition of things to come midway through his second round. Pulling his drive left, he bent over to pull the tee out of the ground and looked up in plenty of time to catch a glimpse of his

After hitting the 18th green in two shots, Jack Nicklaus waves to the cheering crowd as he approaches his eagle putt.

future. There, on the fieldstone porch of a home along the 11th tee, two men in comfortable lawn chairs stared back. The U.S. Open was about to become a spectator sport for the man who played it better than any other.

After shooting a fog-delayed 73 in the first round, Nicklaus began to play like a 60-year-old grandfather of 11 in the second. He double-bogeyed the par-3 fifth, a hole of his design, and slowly his score bled away.

"This wasn't supposed to be the last day," said Nicklaus' dutiful wife Barbara, also making her last Open walk. "We were supposed to be here two more days."

So this was to be his valedictory in the Open, the tournament that really launched him, back in 1962, at Oakmont, when he was the despised Fat Jack,

Jack Nicklaus II provides a towel as his father wipes away tears. In fact, blurred vision would cause Nicklaus to top his eagle putt, leaving the ball 10 feet short on No. 18.

After leaving his second putt on the 18th hole inches short of the cup, Jack Nicklaus provides some comic relief.

unseating The King, Arnold Palmer. When Nicklaus arrived at the 18th tee box, a ledge of turf hanging over the lapping waters of Carmel Bay, he had played 2,897 holes in 44 Open

> ***He had never played a hole like this one. The sun had thoroughly burned away the fog to light up center stage for him one last time.***

come in the play-off against Palmer. Another 18 made up the final-round 65 he shot to win the 1967 Open at Baltusrol. So many of them came at Pebble Beach, where he lived out his dreams, winning the 1972 Open and losing a heartbreaker to Tom Watson 10 years later.

But he had never played a hole like this one. The sun had thoroughly burned away the fog to light up center stage for him one last time. Resplendent and bathed in grace, he hoisted his left leg and half-sat on a sturdy wooden fence along the back of the 18th tee, gazing out upon the glorious setting as the sailboats gently rocked and ripples quietly lapped the shore.

Normally, Nicklaus would hit a 3-wood off the tee on the 548-yard par 5. But today would be different. "I haven't tried to reach this green in two shots in 20 years," he told his son, Jackie, who was on the bag that day. "Let's try."

He ripped a tee shot into the distance, cutting off a slice of Carmel Bay in the process, and wound up in the middle of the fairway. When Nicklaus reached his ball, he was 238 yards from the front of the green, 261 yards from the hole. He faced a terrifying second shot to the green with the seawater closing in on the left side of the green, and a giant pine guarding the right.

For a moment, though, it was 1972 all over again. Nicklaus' hair was blonder, and he was 20 pounds thinner. Bogeys were afraid of *him*.

Nicklaus tore into a 3-wood, hanging his approach shot against the blue sky. He had reached way, way back into his memory and somehow was able to come up with a glorious, final, ringingly defiant smash that hit short of the green, bounced through a narrow opening and came to rest 50 feet from the cup.

Jack Nicklaus II gets a Bear hug from his legendary father. Though his second-round 82 precluded Nicklaus and his son from reaching a Father's Day final, he did complete his 44th and final Open in grand style.

Nicklaus gives his wife a kiss after making their final U.S. Open walk together. "That's the end of it," he told her.

It was then that all heaven broke loose.

Everyone within 500 yards was cheering, including past Open champions Watson, Tom Kite, and Hale Irwin. All three had their own greatness measured against Nicklaus, and were in some way defined by him. Now they returned the compliment, cheering from the middle of the fairway in the group behind the Golden Bear.

Nicklaus took his time getting to the green. He took off his cap, and playfully asked if it was his ball on the putting surface. With magic in the air, his son assisted him in wiping away tears as he stood over his eagle putt.

"Pick it up!" someone yelled from the crowd. "It's good!"

Nicklaus topped the putt, leaving it 10-feet short.

"My eyes were blurry and I was going through the moment," Nicklaus said. "And I whiffed the darned thing."

Ultimately, he would three-putt. "A par on 18 at Pebble. That ain't so bad," Nicklaus said.

He embraced his son, then walked over to his wife behind the green to say the five hardest words of his career.

"That's the end of it."

David Gossett & Don Pooley

After figuratively following in Jack Nicklaus' footsteps, David Gossett did so literally at the conclusion of the second round of the 100th U.S. Open.

Gossett won the 1999 U.S. Amateur at Pebble Beach, nearly 40 years after Nicklaus accomplished the feat. As was the case when Nicklaus won in 1961, Gossett was wondering if this was the right time to start a professional golf career. For Nicklaus, the answer had been an affirmative, as he won his first Open in 1962, beating Arnold Palmer in a play-off at Oakmont Country Club.

After 44 starts, 160 rounds, and 35 cuts made, Jack Nicklaus called it a U.S. Open career in 2000, with the 21-year-old Gossett wide-eyed and in tow as his playing partner.

"I won't be remembered for what I shot today," said Gossett, who was 13-over par for two days and missed the cut. "But I'll always remember this. Always."

By winning the U.S. Amateur, Gossett was awarded a spot in the Open's premier group, which annually consists of the previous year's Open, Amateur, and British Open champions. Nicklaus took the place of the late Payne Stewart.

Gossett's Mitty-esque experience was matched step for step by Don Pooley, the unlikely third member of the premier group. The journeyman pro was flown in from Rockville, Md., on Tuesday to substitute for British Open champion Paul Lawrie, who withdrew from the 2000 Open with a groin injury.

"I went from being an alternate to being a party to history," said Pooley, 48. "Not bad."

Both Gossett and Pooley said they remained silent as Nicklaus took his final walk up the 18th fairway — that is, until the Golden Bear sank his final putt.

Pooley removed his cap and took Nicklaus' hand. "Say it ain't so," he said.

CHAPTER ELEVEN

Open and Shut

A brilliant Saturday performance by Tiger Woods left little to the imagination, and signified that golf desperately needed a rivalry.

Tiger Woods drives off 18 at the conclusion of his second round Saturday and watches his ball splash into the Pacific. It was one of the few missed shots during his march to victory. A frustrated Woods filled the air with curses that were captured on live television. He later apologized for the controversial remarks.

Sergio Garcia jumps up to watch his second shot on the eighth hole Saturday.

The unthinkable

On Saturday, it finally happened.

Tiger Woods had teased the field for the better part of three days at the 100th U.S. Open. Now, they had him right where they wanted him.

In trouble.

Having already absorbed a triple-bogey 7 on the normally benign third hole, Woods found himself buried in a dense nest of grass atop the lip of a fairway bunker on the par-5 sixth hole. The normally suave Woods looked uncharacteristically disheveled, as he had to hit the blind, curling, uphill shot with one foot in the rough and another in the sand. Just wanting to get the shot on the green, Woods chopped it out to the front of the putting surface and watched it roll up and settle eight feet from the flagstick — an unthinkable play.

One could almost hear the 155 other players in the field mutter a collective "Drat!"

A day away

If the goal was to beat the entire golf world into submission, Woods was almost there. Already the world's top player, he'd raised his own level of play beyond what many felt would be his omega point, and in the process was making the planet's top marksmen seem uncomfortable and unworthy. He was the world's best driver, best iron player, best chipper and best putter. And he had an unthinkable 10-shot lead going into the Open's final round, grinding out an even-par 71 in Saturday's third frame to leave a yawning chasm between him and the field. He had reached 8-under par through three rounds, while the best anyone else could manage was 2-over.

The list of records he set in completing both his second and third rounds on Saturday was astonishing. His six-stroke advantage over the field after 36 holes broke a 97-year-old Open record. The previous 36-hole record was five strokes by Willie Anderson in 1903. His total of 134 after 36 holes matched the Open record held by Nicklaus (1980 at Baltusrol), T.C. Chen (1985 at Oakland Hills) and Lee Janzen (1993 at Baltusrol). Lastly, Woods' 10-stroke advantage after 54 holes was the largest ever by a margin of three strokes. The previous record of seven was set by James Barnes in 1921 at Columbia Country Club.

Spectators filling a grandstand along the eighth fairway watch as Tiger Woods attempts to reach the green from atop a 150-foot cliff.

While Javier Sanchez watches from the 10th fairway, surfers catch waves along Carmel Beach.

Master class

No one had dominated a major championship like this since ...well, Tiger Woods.

Comparisons to Woods' triumph at the 1997 Masters — where he led by nine shots after three rounds — were inevitable. But by his own account, the body of work he was culling together at the Open was clearly more impressive.

"It surprises me in the fact that I'm doing this at the U.S. Open," said Woods, who ended up winning the Masters by 12 strokes. "Just because a U.S. Open is very difficult to go low. Don't get me wrong, at Augusta it's difficult to go low, but you can see it's possible because there was no rough and you could hit bombs away.

"I think I've played better this year than I did in 1997, just because it's so much more difficult off the tee at Pebble. At the Masters in 1997, there was no rough, so you could hit the driver as hard as you wanted to and have it get in the fairway. (Augusta) was tailor-made for me that year, so much so that they altered it a lot after I won."

That Woods could consider Saturday a triumph at all was remarkable, considering he tallied four bogeys and a triple in 24 holes, not to mention spewing a sulfuric rant caught on national television after pulling his tee shot on No. 18 into the water at the completion of his second round. The incident was made worse by the fact that NBC had preempted cartoons that morning to give expanded Open coverage, thus making children privy to the curses.

"It was the heat of the moment," Woods said. "I'm one of those guys who plays pretty intense, and unfortunately I let it slip out, and I regret doing it."

A shot in the arm

Some thought the rest of the field could have used a dose of Woods' intensity. Jim Furyk shot 84, Hal Sutton 83, and Sergio Garcia 81. The lone impressive performance was posted by Ernie Els, who went 3-under par Saturday to reach 2-over for the tournament, good enough for second place.

"It was probably one of the best rounds I've ever played in major golf," Els said, "and I'm still kind of embarrassed."

Phil Mickelson and David Duval, who couldn't break par in their collective six rounds on a course where Woods had done it twice, expressed a similar inability to make up the necessary ground to catch Tiger.

Indeed, despite Woods' mockery of par, and the 11-percent increase in television viewership over the 1999 U.S. Open, some were left wondering what was once unimaginable: Was Tiger Woods good for golf?

Colin Montgomerie

Making his U.S. Open debut at Pebble Beach in 1992, Colin Montgomerie went into the clubhouse as the fourth-round leader with a Sunday 70 in ungodly conditions. He was immediately whisked up to the TV tower, where he received the golf equivalent of a papal blessing.

"Congratulations on your first Open title," no less an authority than Jack Nicklaus said to Montgomerie.

"I must admit, I thought at the last hole, I was putting to win the tournament," Montgomerie reflected. "Think about how different things would be..."

Of course, Tom Kite went on to win the championship, beginning Montgomerie's ignominious career at Pebble Beach, and in the United States. Despite a run of strong U.S. Open appearances — he made the cut in all nine of his starts, with second-place finishes in 1994 and 1997 — Montgomerie realized the American national title was one he'd not likely win.

"American galleries and I tend to not get along," Montgomerie said. The combustible Montgomerie argued openly with the crowd at the 1998 U.S. Open at Olympic Club, and the chiding grew so strong at the 1999 Ryder Cup in Brookline, MA, that Montgomerie's father, an esteemed golf official, had to be removed from the scene.

The environment was typically rancorous during second- and third-round play at Pebble Beach, where the maligned Scotsman, despite traveling with a coterie of Monterey County deputies, was ridiculed by gallery members calling him "Mrs. Doubtfire" and "Fool Monty." The chiding ended up delaying play, as the offending fans were taken from the course.

"Unfortunately, it's getting worse instead of better," Montgomerie said. "It's become blood sport."

Marshals stand watch on the ninth hole as a fishing boat cruises by in the background on Saturday.

A group of New Zealanders don Dr. Seuss-like hats in honor of their favorite cat, Tiger Woods.

While Woods' domination was awe-inspiring, one had to hope the rest of the field was not truly 10-strokes worse. If Woods was 10 strokes better than everyone else based on talent alone, golf would blossom the way it did when Arnold Palmer hitched his pants and took the game to new levels of popularity.

But the fear was that what separated Woods from the pack had more to do with desire.

"That hunger for winning a major championship...it's there every time," Els said. "To be honest with you, I don't feel like that every week I'm playing. Whether it's a tournament or a major, he's going to be 110 percent."

What golf needed was a rivalry. What would Magic have been without Bird? Chamberlin without Russell? The Steelers without the Cowboys? McEnroe without Connors?

"I liken it to when Arnold Palmer came along," Jack Nicklaus said. "Arnold came along after Snead, Hogan and Nelson were all past their prime. There was a five, six, seven-year gap where not much happened. Nobody dominated, then Arnold came along when the public needed someone. Then Gary (Player) came along, then I came along.

"Right now there's nobody contending. Vijay Singh has won two majors. Ernie Els has won two. That would be the closest. I was playing Arnold, who won seven, Gary nine, Lee Trevino six, Tom Watson eight.

"Tiger is good for the game, as Arnie was. But it only works long term if you have challengers to make the thing right. The game is at its apex now. But should a Duval, a Mickelson, an Els rise up, boy, the sky's the limit."

For now, however, NBC had an interesting piece of programming on its hands for Sunday — six hours of exhibition golf.

Top: *Playing partner Thomas Bjorn's expression reflects the field's frustration in catching Woods. "The score is honest," he said. "How do I make up 10 strokes?"*

Above: *Tiger Woods would drive television viewership up 11 percent over the 1999 U.S. Open.*

CHAPTER TWELVE

Beauty *and* *the* Beach

*With a record-shattering 15-shot win,
Tiger Woods completed the most dominating
performance in golf history.*

Tiger Woods and caddie Steve Williams discuss Woods' strategy at the outset of the first round. At 8-under, Woods would need to gain three more shots on par to tie Willie Smith's U.S. Open record of 11-under set in 1899.

Tiger Woods and Ernie Els chat on the first tee prior to Sunday's final round. Els' 3-under 68 had been the best individual round Saturday.

A game of perfect

If a person can be judged by the company he keeps, what can be said of a man without peer?

"Those who know golf understand that it is a game that consists far more of small failures than of success," Ernie Els said. "Someone said, 'Golf is not a game of perfect.' But if Tiger Woods wasn't perfect here this week, in this perfect place, then I don't know that the word should exist."

On a crystalline, sun-speckled Sunday, in a golf kingdom by the sea surrounded by unsurpassed primal wonder, Woods completed the most dominating four-round performance in the history of championship golf.

Above the Cliffs of Doom, around Stillwater Cove and Carmel Bay, along the seawall of the Pacific, in the shadows of cypress trees draped in Spanish moss, the 24-year-old put on a show of power and precision, patience and panache, and won the 100th U.S. Open championship by a devastating 15 strokes.

In the process he overwhelmed the very finest players on the planet, routing Americans and Brits, Spaniards and Scots, South Africans and Danes, Irishmen and Swedes.

In the Open, par is, and has always been, the sacred score. But Woods toured 72 holes at the game's cathedral in 12 strokes under par. He shot, in succession, 65-69-71-67. One golfer suggested that the putting surfaces at Pebble Beach had become so dry as to turn purple. Perhaps the course was merely blushing.

"Tiger has raised the bar," said Tom Watson, who won his only U.S. Open at Pebble Beach in 1982, "and it seems that he's the only guy who can jump over that bar."

"We always felt someone would come along who could drive the ball 300 yards and putt like Ben Crenshaw," Nick Price said. "This guy drives the ball further than anybody I've ever seen and putts better than Crenshaw. He's a phenomenon."

Woods' winning margin was two strokes better than the record for a major championship set back in '62 — 1862, that is, by Old Tom Morris, who accomplished

All eyes are on Tiger Woods Sunday, who was 17-2 lifetime when heading into the final round with a lead. Though the outcome was never in doubt, NBC reported television viewership Sunday increased nearly 20 percent over the previous year's Open.

Bobby Clampett, hitting from the cliffs above Monterey Bay in the final round of his Open homecoming, would finish with a 68-77-76-77-298.

the feat at the British Open against a field of 12 players. The 15-stroke victory was four better than the previous U.S. Open record, established by Willie Smith in 1899.

> *"If Tiger Woods wasn't perfect here this week, in this perfect place, then I don't know that the word should exist."*
>
> — Ernie Els

When the sun set on the Monterey Peninsula Sunday night, Woods also held championship records for the largest lead after 36 holes (six strokes), lowest 36-hole score (134, tied with Jack Nicklaus, T.C. Chen, and Lee Janzen), largest 54-hole lead (10), lowest 72-hole score (272, tied with Nicklaus and Janzen), and most strokes under par at any time (12, tied with Gil Morgan).

The magnitude of his victory can best be understood when considering the following: If one were to add together the margin of victory of all the Open winners in the 1990s, it would not equal Woods' margin in 2000.

Final round

With his final round Sunday, Woods established himself as the possessor of an invulnerable game, the best at whatever shot is required and at exercising an unbendable force of will.

Woods reported to the first tee with a 10-stroke advantage. To date, Woods had been uncatchable when he had a lead in his teeth; his record when leading after 54 holes was 17-2. While most would have enjoyed the 18-hole victory lap, it was clear his intent was to make history. Woods took dead aim at the record books and went after them with clinical fury.

He made nine consecutive pars on the opening nine, then made his play on the backside. He birdied 10, 12, 13, and 14, taking his score to 12-under. As had been the case all week, he never three-putted.

"I watched the scoreboard in total wonderment," admitted Padraig Harrington, the Irishman who finished in fifth place by an outlandish margin of 17 strokes.

In posting his 12th victory in his last 21 starts, Woods became the first wire-to-wire winner at the U.S. Open since Payne Stewart in 1991, and the eighth in the championship's history. It gave him the third leg in the career Grand Slam, and in a month he would attempt to join Nicklaus, Gene Sarazen, Ben Hogan, and Gary Player as the only golfers to win the U.S. Open, Masters, British Open, and PGA Championship.

Tom Watson

Tom Watson took a ride in the time machine during the final round of his 29th — and perhaps last — U.S. Open.

Watson's trip down memory lane came when his tee shot landed in the rough left of the flagstick on No. 17. It was almost the same spot from where he launched his miraculous birdie chip-in to defeat Jack Nicklaus in the 1982 Open.

"When the ball ended up left of the green, Bruce (Edwards), my caddie (who also caddied for Watson in '82), said, 'No! I can't believe that — not again!' This was a little different situation, obviously."

It was a different result, too. This time, Watson did as Edwards suggested 18 years ago — he merely got it close, but not close enough to avoid bogey. And although Watson birdied 18 — as he also did in '82 to lock up the two-stroke win over Nicklaus — the final-round 73 left him at 296, in 27th place and three strokes shy of automatic qualifying for the 2001 Open at Southern Hills in Tulsa, Okla.

Thus, Watson's incredible Open run, which began the first time Pebble Beach hosted the championship in 1972, likely came to an unceremonious conclusion. In all, he completed 104 Open rounds and missed only six cuts in 29 events. He won eight majors, including five British Opens, and from 1975-83 rivaled Nicklaus as the world's best player.

"I'm eternally grateful for what the Open has given me," Watson said, blinking back tears. "My Open win at Pebble in '82, and the big shot on 17, has afforded me more friends than I can count. Probably in the stands that day, there were around 1,500 people. But I've had, over the course of 18 years, probably 6,000 to 10,000 people tell me they were there."

Opposite page: *Tiger Woods grimaces as his birdie putt skims the cup on No. 3. Woods made nine straight pars to start the fourth round.*

Above: *Red numbers, and an enterprising fan, complete Tiger Woods' Sunday scoring line.*

Right: *There was another Tiger getting his share of attention as Billy Bird donned a catty costume for the big event.*

Tiger Woods tees off on 18 during the final round of the U.S. Open. At 12-under par, 15 strokes ahead of the field, just one hole lay between him and history.

Opposite page: *Woods acknowledges the crowd as he makes the walk up 18 on his way to a landslide victory.*

Top: *Fans in the 18th hole grandstand cheer Woods as he approaches the green.*

Far left: *Wood's gives his signature fist pump after sinking his putt on 18. His 15-shot margin of victory would break a record set in 1862 during the Lincoln administration.*

Left: *Woods is congratulated by his caddie Steve Williams.*

Tiger Woods shares his moment of glory with his mother, Tida.

Woods embraces his coach, Butch Harmon.

Legend in his own time

From the outset, the other 155 players in the Open field were playing against Woods, and Woods alone.

"To me, the ultimate compliment in sports is that you want to know where that person is on the field all the time, no matter if they have the ball or not," said Tom Lehman, who finished 23 shots behind Woods. "To tell the truth, we're always looking on the scoreboard to see what he's doing. If it were me who had gotten ahead, maybe we would have been more patient trying to catch up. But when (Woods) gets four or five or six shots ahead, you stop playing patient golf and then it makes the gap widen even more."

Watching with their jaws wide open were a number of the world's Top 10 players, including David Duval (19 strokes back), Masters champion Vijay Singh (19 strokes back), Phil Mickelson (21 strokes back), Hal Sutton (23 strokes back), Colin Montgomerie (27 strokes back) and Davis Love III (missed cut).

Told that he led the tournament in fairways hit, Montgomerie shot back, "That's great. They should put the hole in the fairway."

The traditional front runners were replaced by a cadre of Europeans, putting to rest years of futility for players from across the pond. Spain's Miguel Angel Jimenez tied Els for second place, with England's Lee Westwood and Padraig Harrington tied for fifth.

Instead of challenging these mortals, however, Woods' performance catapulted him into an echelon where he could only compete against perfection — and ghosts. While the rest of the field played Woods, he played the likes of Bobby Jones, Byron Nelson, Arnold Palmer, and Jack Nicklaus.

But Arnie would have required more than an army to challenge Woods, and Nelson would have needed two strokes a side. Woods proved to be the rarest of athletic birds — the supremely talented overachiever, melding supreme gifts with well-honed mechanics. Ben Hogan's swing was so flat he looked more like DiMaggio, Nicklaus had the flying right elbow, and Palmer was all arms and heart. But Woods' swing had become a singular, balletic piece of majesty.

Woods was paid the ultimate compliment by longtime golf writer Dan Jenkins. After watching Woods shoot his fourth round of par or better on a course that had yielded only 32 subpar rounds to the rest of the field, Jenkins said, "I saw him do things this week that I never saw Hogan do."

Even comparisons to Nicklaus began to ring hollow. At the 2000 Open, Woods beat everyone in the field on three of four days. Nicklaus, on the other hand, played in 44 Opens and beat the rest of the field only once in any round.

"I had my century," Nicklaus said. "Let Tiger have the 21st."

Tiger Woods admires the U.S. Open trophy.

Stephanie and Mike Tollison of Oklahoma City snap a souvenir photo on the 18th green, one day after Tiger Woods' 15-stroke win shook the sports world.

Afterword

It would have been nice to experience Jones or Hogan, though you realize you might not have appreciated it at the time, as your sense of history heightens on the follow-through. But to watch what Tiger Woods did at the 100th U.S. Open was to experience the Next Big Thing — the sporting equivalent of seeing Michelangelo mix colors — and Pebble Beach was Florence at the beginning of the Renaissance. As if it weren't indulgent enough to fall in love with the place for its beauty alone, now Woods had made it his canvas.

In retrospect, it was never really about beating Duval, Sergio or Mickelson, Vijay, Monty or Davis Love. Though arguably the most talented group of contenders in the game's history, they rightfully existed in Woods' peripheral vision. No, this was about Woods facing the daunting task of walking into the immense shadow of his own evolving lore. Despite his awesome physical prowess and water-to-wine miracle comebacks — including the one he staged at Pebble Beach in February when he won the AT&T Pro-Am despite being down seven strokes with seven holes to play — he could not get ahead of his own legend.

This one was for immortality. St. Andrews may be the birthplace of golf, but Pebble Beach is where Woods laid the game as we knew it to rest.

The 100th U.S. Open left sports historians scrambling. What was more impressive, 7 or 15? And to what do we compare a 15-stroke victory? Should it be put up against aberrations in time, like Secretariat's 31-length victory at the Belmont Stakes in 1973, Bob Beamon leaping more than 29 feet at the 1968 Olympics, or Wilt Chamberlin's 100 point night? Or was it more a testament to revolutionary athleticism distilled over a period of time, like Babe Ruth, whose 60 home runs in 1927 exceeded the total of any other American League team, or Mark Spitz swimming to seven gold medals?

A month after Pebble Beach, Woods traveled to the Old Course at St. Andrews and won the British Open, at 24 becoming the youngest among five winners of the career Grand Slam. Moreover, he rightfully joined Ruth, Ali, and Jordan as the four horsemen of sport, men who would be bigger than the games they played; global athletes who could take a pastime and move it to preoccupation. Though their skills would be harbingers of thunder, silence could be their style, quiet their currency. If victory lurked somewhere within a microbe's cunning, they would track it down, ever the sweet scientists. Each possessed a visceral ability — Ruth's power, Ali's speed, Jordan's flight, Woods' adrenaline — that made exaggeratedly human onlookers feel a part of the action nonetheless.

As was the case with the other three, Woods will someday have his heavyweight glory behind him, his bittersweet future beckoning him to step into it. At that point, he can reflect on the sentiment felt by those at Pebble Beach for the 100th U.S. Open: It was a pleasure to be in his time.

100 Champions

1895 - Horace Rawlins, Newport G.C.
1896 - James Foulis, Shinnecock Hills G.C.
1897 - Joe Lloyd, Chicago G.C.
1898 - Fred Herd, Myopia Hunt Club
1899 - Willie Smith, Baltimore C.C.
1900 - Harry Vardon, Chicago G.C.
1901 - Willie Anderson, Myopia Hunt Club
1902 - Lawrence Auchterlonie, Garden City G.C.
1903 - Willie Anderson, Baltusrol G.C.
1904 - Willie Anderson, Glen View Club
1905 - Willie Anderson, Myopia Hunt Club
1906 - Alex Smith, Onwentsia Club
1907 - Alex Ross, Philadelphia Cricket Club
1908 - Fred McLeod, Myopia Hunt Club
1909 - George Sargent, Englewood G.C.
1910 - Alex Smith, Philadelphia Cricket Club
1911 - John J. McDermott, Chicago G.C.
1912 - John J. McDermott, Country Club of Buffalo
1913 - Francis Ouimet, The Country Club (MA)
1914 - Walter Hagen, Midlothian C.C.
1915 - Jerome D. Travers, Baltusrol G.C.
1916 - Charles Evans Jr., Minikahda Club
1917-18 - No Championships: World War I
1919 - Walter Hagen, Brae Burn C.C.
1920 - Edward Ray, Inverness Club
1921 - James M. Barnes, Columbia C.C.
1922 - Gene Sarazen, Skokie C.C.
1923 - Robert T. Jones, Inwood C.C.
1924 - Cyril Walker, Oakland Hills C.C.
1925 - William McFarlane, Worcester C.C.
1926 - Robert T. Jones, Scioto C.C.
1927 - Tommy Armour, Oakmont C.C.
1928 - Johnny Farrell, Olympia Fields C.C.
1929 - Robert T. Jones, Winged Foot G.C.
1930 - Robert T. Jones, Interlachen C.C.
1931 - Billy Burke, Inverness Club
1932 - Gene Sarazen, Fresh Meadow C.C.
1933 - John Goodman, North Shore G.C.
1934 - Olin Dutra, Merion Cricket Club
1935 - Sam Parks Jr., Oakmont C.C.
1936 - Tony Manero, Baltusrol G.C.
1937 - Ralph Guldahl, Oakland Hills G.C.
1938 - Ralph Guldahl, Cherry Hills Club

1939 - Byron Nelson, Philadelphia C.C.
1940 - Lawson Little, Canterbury G.C.
1941 - Craig Wood, Colonial C.C.
1942-45 - No Championships: World War II
1946 - Lloyd Mangrum, Canterbury G.C.
1947 - Lew Worsham, St. Louis C.C.
1948 - Ben Hogan, Riviera C.C.
1949 - Cary Middlecoff, Medinah C.C.
1950 - Ben Hogan, Merion G.C.
1951 - Ben Hogan, Oakland Hills
1952 - Julius Boros, Northwood Club
1953 - Ben Hogan, Oakmont C.C.
1954 - Ed Furgol, Baltusrol G.C.
1955 - Jack Fleck, Olympic Club
1956 - Cary Middlecoff, Oak Hill C.C.
1957 - Dick Mayer, Inverness Club
1958 - Tommy Bolt, Southern Hills
1959 - Bill Casper Jr., Winged Foot
1960 - Arnold Palmer, Cherry Hills C.C.
1961 - Gene Littler, Oakland Hills C.C.
1962 - Jack Nicklaus, Oakmont C.C.
1963 - Julius Boros, The Country Club (Mass.)
1964 - Ken Venturi, Congressional C.C.
1965 - Gary Player, Bellerive C.C.
1966 - Bill Casper Jr., Olympic Club
1967 - Jack Nicklaus, Baltusrol G.C.
1968 - Lee Trevino, Oak Hill C.C.
1969 - Orville Moody, Champions G.C.
1970 - Tony Jacklin, Hazeltine National
1971 - Lee Trevino, Merion G.C.
1972 - Jack Nicklaus, Pebble Beach G.L.
1973 - Johnny Miller, Oakmont C.C.
1974 - Hale Irwin, Winged Foot G.C.
1975 - Lou Graham, Medinah C.C.
1976 - Jerry Pate, Atlanta Athletic Club
1977 - Hubert Green, Southern Hills C.C.
1978 - Andy North, Cherry Hills C.C.
1979 - Hale Irwin, Inverness Club
1980 - Jack Nicklaus, Baltusrol G.C.
1981 - David Graham, Merion G.C.
1982 - Tom Watson, Pebble Beach G.L.
1983 - Larry Nelson, Oakmont C.C.
1984 - Fuzzy Zoeller, Winged Foot G.C.
1985 - Andy North, Oakland Hills C.C.
1986 - Raymond Floyd, Shinnecock Hills G.C.

1987 - Scott Simpson, Olympic Club
1988 - Curtis Strange, The Country Club (MA)
1989 - Curtis Strange, Oak Hill C.C.
1990 - Hale Irwin, Medinah C.C.
1991 - Payne Stewart, Hazeltine National
1992 - Tom Kite, Pebble Beach G.L.
1993 - Lee Janzen, Baltusrol G.C.
1994 - Ernie Els, Oakmont C.C.
1995 - Corey Pavin, Shinnecock Hills G.C.
1996 - Steve Jones, Oakland Hills C.C.
1997 - Ernie Els, Congressional C.C.
1998 - Lee Janzen, Olympic Club
1999 - Payne Stewart, Pinehurst No. 2
2000 - Tiger Woods, Pebble Beach G.L.

Photo Credits

Pg. 1, Orville Myers
Pg. 3, Vern Fisher
Pg. 4, Cole Thompson
Pg. 6, Orville Myers
Pg. 8, Orville Myers
Pg. 10, Vern Fisher
Pg. 12, Cole Thompson
Pg. 14, Orville Myers
Pg. 16, Vern Fisher
Pg. 18, Associated Press file photo
Pg. 20, Associated Press file photo
Pg. 21, Associated Press file photo
Pg. 22, Associated Press file photo
Pg. 23, Associated Press file photo
Pg. 24, Cole Thompson
Pg. 26, Cole Thompson
Pg. 27, upper right, Orville Myers
Pg. 27, bottom, Cole Thompson
Pg. 28, Vern Fisher
Pg. 30, Vern Fisher
Pg. 32, Christine Thompson
Pg. 34, Vern Fisher
Pg. 35, Orville Myers
Pg. 36, Orville Myers
Pg. 38, Orville Myers
Pg. 39, Vern Fisher
Pg. 40, Cole Thompson
Pg. 41, Vern Fisher
Pg. 42, top, Orville Myers
Pg. 42, bottom, Cole Thompson
Pg. 43, Cole Thompson
Pg. 44, Cole Thompson
Pg. 46, Cole Thompson
Pg. 47, Cole Thompson
Pg. 48, Vern Fisher
Pg. 49, Vern Fisher
Pg. 50, Vern Fisher
Pg. 52, Vern Fisher
Pg. 54, Vern Fisher
Pg. 55, Orville Myers
Pg. 56, Vern Fisher
Pg. 58, Orville Myers
Pg. 59, Orville Myers
Pg. 60, Orville Myers
Pg. 61, Christine Thompson
Pg. 62, Vern Fisher
Pg. 63, Vern Fisher
Pg. 64, Vern Fisher
Pg. 65, Vern Fisher
Pg. 66, Vern Fisher
Pg. 68, Orville Myers
Pg. 69, top, Vern Fisher
Pg. 69, bottom, Orville Myers
Pg. 70, Vern Fisher
Pg. 72, Orville Myers

Pg. 73, Orville Myers
Pg. 74, Vern Fisher
Pg. 75, Cole Thompson
Pg. 76, Cole Thompson
Pg. 77, Cole Thompson
Pg. 78, Orville Myers
Pg. 80, Cole Thompson
Pg. 81, Cole Thompson
Pg. 82, Orville Myers
Pg. 83, Cole Thompson
Pg. 84, Vern Fisher
Pg. 85, Cole Thompson
Pg. 86, Cole Thompson
Pg. 87, USGA staff photo
Pg. 88, Vern Fisher
Pg. 90, Christine Thompson
Pg. 91, Cole Thompson
Pg. 92, Christine Thompson
Pg. 94, Orville Myers
Pg. 95, top and right photos, Cole Thompson
Pg. 95, center, Orville Myers
Pg. 96, Associated Press file photo
Pg. 97, Vern Fisher
Pg. 98, Cole Thompson
Pg. 100, top and left, Cole Thompson
Pg. 100, right, Orville Myers
Pg. 101, Cole Thompson
Pg. 102, top, Cole Thompson
Pg. 102, left, Clay Peterson
Pg. 102, right, Orville Myers
Pg. 103, Vern Fisher
Pg. 104, Christine Thompson
Pg. 106, Orville Myers
Pg. 107, Orville Myers
Pg. 108, Vern Fisher
Pg. 110, Vern Fisher
Pg. 111, Cole Thompson
Pg. 112, Vern Fisher
Pg. 114, top, Vern Fisher
Pg. 114, bottom, Christine Thompson
Pg. 115, Christine Thompson
Pg. 116, top, Vern Fisher
Pg. 116, bottom, Cole Thompson
Pg. 117, Christine Thompson
Pg. 118, Vern Fisher
Pg. 120, top, Christine Thompson
Pg. 120, bottom, Orville Myers
Pg. 121, Christine Thompson
Pg. 122, Vern Fisher
Pg. 124, top and right, Vern Fisher
Pg. 124, left, Cole Thompson
Pg. 125, Vern Fisher
Pg. 126, Vern Fisher
Pg. 128, Cole Thompson
Pg. 129, Orville Myers